Praise for

SQUANDERED

"A significant contribution to thinking about resource policy."
—**JIM STANFORD**, Economist and Director, Centre for Future Work

"A penetrating analysis of how successive Saskatchewan governments failed to claim the potash wealth owed to the people of the province."
—**DALE EISLER**, *From Left to Right*

"Eric Cline has written an important book that should outrage all Saskatchewan citizens. He documents, in meticulous detail, the billions of dollars Saskatchewan has lost through poor resource royalty structures, financial giveaways, and other deals to the benefit of Potash producers and their shareholders at the expense of the provincial treasury."
—**KEN RASMUSSEN**, Director of Johnson-Shoyama Graduate School of Public Policy, University of Regina

"Eric Cline is much like a Saskatchewan mid-winter blizzard—powerful, impressive, unpredictable, and impactful. His distinguished career as a politician, cabinet minister, corporate executive, and all-around great provincial citizen has earned him the right to speak frankly and authoritatively on the major policy and economic issues in Saskatchewan. This provocative, well-argued, and important book raises the curtain on the province's world-class potash industry. *Squandered* reveals that there is a great deal of money, power, and policy behind the potash slag heaps that are rapidly replacing grain elevators as the talismans of Saskatchewan's prosperity. Eric Cline's thoughtful analysis is destined to become a standard work on the political economy of this province."
—**KEN COATES**, Canada Research Chair in Regional Innovation, University of Saskatchewan

"The Canadian prairies were settled to provide the world with a 'breadbasket.' Ever since, the settlers living there have been looking to diversify. They found remarkable bounties. And then...at key moments, feckless provincial governments were captured by private interests, who then transferred this wealth to themselves. That's how oil-rich Alberta came

to be in net debt, while Norway accumulated a trillion-dollar wealth fund. And that is how potash-rich Saskatchewan also had its family silver quietly pocketed. Eric Cline understands what a tragic, once-in-history lost opportunity this is for the people of Saskatchewan. He lived the consequences as Finance Minister. He tells this enraging and outrageous tale in this book. Which might just persuade you it's time for a change."
—**BRIAN TOPP**, Max Bell School of Public Policy, McGill University

SQUANDERED
CANADA'S POTASH LEGACY

ERIC CLINE

Printed and bound in Canada at Marquis Book Printing. The text of this book is printed on 100% post-consumer recycled paper with earth-friendly vegetable-based inks.

Cover art: "Tunnel of deep potash mine." by Elena Bionysheva-Abramova / iStock Photo
Cover design: Duncan Campbell, University of Regina Press
Interior layout design: John van der Woude, JVDW Designs
Copyeditor: Adrineh Der-Boghossian
Proofreader: Shannon Parr
Indexer: Judy Dunlop

Library and Archives Canada Cataloguing in Publication

Title: Squandered : Canada's potash legacy / Eric Cline.
Names: Cline, Eric, 1955- author.
Description: Includes bibliographical references and index.
Identifiers: Canadiana (print) 20230548164 | Canadiana (ebook) 20230548210 | ISBN 9780889779693 (softcover) | ISBN 9780889779716 (EPUB) | ISBN 9780889779709 (PDF)
Subjects: LCSH: Potash industry and trade—Saskatchewan. | LCSH: Potash mines and mining—Saskatchewan.
Classification: LCC HD9660.P7 C3 2024 | DDC 338.2/7636097124—dc23

10 9 8 7 6 5 4 3 2 1

University of Regina Press, University of Regina
Regina, Saskatchewan, Canada, S4S 0A2
TEL: (306) 585-4758 FAX: (306) 585-4699
WEB: www.uofrpress.ca

U OF R PRESS

We acknowledge the support of the Canada Council for the Arts for our publishing program. We acknowledge the financial support of the Government of Canada. / Nous reconnaissons l'appui financier du gouvernement du Canada. This publication was made possible with support from Creative Saskatchewan's Book Publishing Production Grant Program.

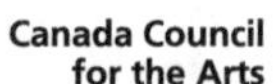

CONTENTS

LIST OF TABLES

PREFACE

Potash is a vital resource. Without it, people go hungry. That fact will become only more important as the world population continues to grow.

A detailed chronicle of the early days of developing Saskatchewan's rich and unparalleled potash resource, as well as the creation and performance of the Potash Corporation of Saskatchewan (PCS), is ably presented in John Burton's *Potash: An Inside Account of Saskatchewan's Pink Gold*, published by the University of Regina Press in 2014.

Some of that history is summarized here to inform and contextualize the discussion of potash mining in Canada in the last few decades. This book's focus is on how the current ownership, operation, and taxation of the potash industry serves the public interest in providing jobs, maximizing economic development in Saskatchewan, and increasing the benefits to the Saskatchewan people from the sale of their potash resource, especially during times of high demand, prices, and profits, as has been the case for the past sixteen years or so.

During my terms as Saskatchewan's minister of finance (1997–2003) and minister of industry and resources (2003–2007), I interacted regularly with potash company executives and was directly involved in all public policy decisions related to the mining sector. After retiring from politics, I worked in the mining sector, including six years as a vice-president of K+S Potash Canada. I also served on the boards of both the Saskatchewan Mining Association and the Saskatchewan Potash Producers' Association.

My perspective as an author is naturally both informed and influenced by my experience as an insider in both public policy-making within government and as a corporate executive in the mining sector, as well by my personal and political views. My perspective is also greatly influenced by the fact that I am a citizen of Saskatchewan and care about its challenges and its future. The primary purpose of this work is not to score political points. Rather, its primary purpose is to present facts in an honest and unvarnished way, which I hope and intend readers from various political perspectives will see to be objective and which will allow them to draw their own conclusions.

Eric Cline
Saskatoon, March 2024

INTRODUCTION

Momentous developments in the potash industry occurred in Saskatchewan in the 1960s under Premier Ross Thatcher, in the 1970s under Premier Allan Blakeney, and in the 1980s under Premier Grant Devine. Nevertheless, more game-changing developments have occurred since then, including unprecedented high demand, prices, and production levels; rejection of efforts by BHP Group Ltd. (BHP) to acquire Potash Corporation of Saskatchewan Inc. (PCS) and its ongoing consequences; and the merger of PCS and Agrium Inc. into the vertically integrated Nutrien Ltd., the world's largest producer and retailer of fertilizer. Arguably, this last development was really the productive capacity of the world's largest producer of potash, PCS, and the majority of Saskatchewan's potash production being absorbed into a fertilizer company needing a cost-effective source of potash, distinct from being a potash miner focused primarily on the business of mining potash.

The story of potash development in Saskatchewan involves discussing competing visions. The Liberal government of Premier Ross Thatcher (1964–1971) accelerated potash mine development, which had begun under the Co-operative Commonwealth Federation/New Democratic Party (CCF/NDP) government of 1956–1964. The NDP government led by Allan Blakeney (1971–1982) concluded the province's interests could best be served through public ownership of part of the potash industry and created the Potash Corporation of Saskatchewan as a Crown corporation. Following the 1989 decision by the Progressive Conservative government of Grant Devine (1982–1991) to place all potash production in private hands, the potash mining industry in Saskatchewan benefitted from steady growth in world market demand, which, by 2006, made the industry enormously profitable. The consolidation of the industry began when PCS purchased five mines. In 2004, Mosaic would emerge as a successor to IMC, which by then owned the two mines it had developed at Esterhazy, and the Belle Plaine and Colonsay operations built by Kalium and Central Canada Potash, respectively. Saskatchewan's potash is an attractive resource to some of the largest pools of world capital. PCS was the target of a hostile takeover bid for that reason. World capital pays attention to a product needed to feed a growing and hungry world population. Saskatchewan has witnessed single mines operating as branch plants that were part of large enterprises engaged in other activities where their focus was not primarily on potash. The province also witnessed government ownership of half of the productive capacity of Saskatchewan's potash mines. Now we have gone to large foreign conglomerates controlling the potash extraction business, and larger ones want a piece of it.

The creation of PCS, its privatization, the explosion of demand for potash, and continued concentration of the industry into a smaller number of players are parts of a fascinating and largely unknown story. Another part of the story involves two competing visions: public enterprise through public ownership of a significant part of potash mining on the one hand, and complete private ownership of the potash industry on the other.

This book sets out to examine the question of how the public interest objectives that led to the creation of the Potash Corporation of Saskatchewan—industry expansion, market decisions influenced by Saskatchewan interests, and maximization of return to the public for the sale of its resource—have been served in this transition.

This book tells the story of early potash mine development in Saskatchewan by nine separate companies; conflict between the industry and the Saskatchewan government; and the creation, privatization, and effective disappearance of the Potash Corporation of Saskatchewan. It recounts the industry consolidating mainly into two major corporations and presents their financial returns from potash as well as the returns to the people of Saskatchewan. It refers to the assessment of experts on whether there is a fair balance between corporate profit and the price paid to the public for their potash resource.

This book's thesis is that there is a gross imbalance between corporate return and public share, to the great detriment of Saskatchewan. It asserts that what the people of the province are being paid for their potash is far below the resource's value. This book asserts that if this imbalance is not corrected, the increasing divide between the wealthy and the poor will continue to grow in Saskatchewan, the tax burden on ordinary people and industries other than potash will be too high, and the overall quality of life in Saskatchewan will go down. As such, the question of how the profits of potash should be shared is the most important question Saskatchewan faces.

The backdrop to the over-sixty-year history of potash mining in Saskatchewan is a longer story, one about hope. Saskatchewan people have always hoped for a future day when heads are held high in a place recognized for its success, self-sufficiency, and heart. They want Saskatchewan to be a place where they can pursue a good life, not just a place they fondly remember or sometimes visit, as they pursue their dreams somewhere else. This book asks whether the potash story is evolving in a way that best achieves what Saskatchewan people have always hoped for.

ONE

THE IMPORTANCE OF POTASH

THE TOPIC OF FOSSIL FUEL CONSUMPTION, IN THE FACE OF VERY real climate change issues, dominates public discussion when questions about natural resources are raised. When Canadians are thinking about the country's natural resources, it's probably fair to say that potash is not top of mind. There is not a high level of awareness that Canada largely controls a key resource that will play a crucial role in determining whether a growing human race gets fed. The issue of food supply, if not properly managed, may well be the cause of catastrophe and war in the coming decades. Canada's Deputy Prime Minister Chrystia Freeland toured a Saskatchewan potash mine in August 2022. She noted that the importance of potash was increasing, but that it had always been important "because it is part of how we feed the people, and nothing is more important than that."[1] She stated that world leaders were paying attention to Canada's potash mines as an alternative to Russian supply, and people around the world were depending on Canada to support democratic allies.[2] Yet Canada has abandoned any significant role in managing the only significant reserves of potash in the free world. Increasingly, control of potash, undeniably necessary to feed the world, has been relinquished mainly to two multinational corporations. The understandable goal of corporate giants mining potash to maximize profit may not by itself best serve the interests of Canada and particularly Saskatchewan, and of humanity's need for more equitable sustenance.

It's time to examine what has been happening in Canada's potash industry and to ask whether this "strategic resource," as the governments of Saskatchewan and Canada have described it, is being developed and exploited in a strategic manner, in terms of economic and policy objectives.

In 2022, BHP, the second-largest mining company in the world, sold its petroleum business for US$2.8 billion[3] and said the capital would go to developing its Jansen potash mine in Saskatchewan. The company's chief financial officer said: "We're replacing our petroleum business with potash."[4] He went on to say that even if potash prices fell by 50 percent from their 2022 level, BHP would "be generating around US$4 to US$5 billion of EBITDA per year. For comparison, our petroleum business averaged around US$3 billion per annum over the past five years."[5]

It seems, therefore, that BHP's US$2.8 billion investment in potash mining will result in much more revenue than oil and gas. If prices remained at 2022 levels, they could make US$5–8 billion based on the estimate as quoted above.

While Canadians have not been paying a lot of attention to their potash resource, the corporate world has been, at the highest levels. BHP saw a commodity that is hot, and getting hotter, and the company is going for it. Referring to interest in Saskatchewan's potash mines, former PCS chief financial officer Wayne Brownlee stated: "We knew the big miners were out there—BHP, Rio Tinto."[6] Agrium effectively absorbed PCS into its vertically integrated global system with the creation of Nutrien in 2018, thereby transferring the world's largest potash miner to a vertically integrated fertilizer giant.[7]

World population is projected to rise from eight billion to nearly ten billion by 2050. That reality, along with higher living standards for some of the world, drives a growing demand for food. A *Harvard Business Review* article asserts: "Food demand is expected to increase anywhere between 59 percent to 98 percent by 2050."[8]

At the same time, the amount of farmable land is estimated to have decreased by about one-third in the last forty years. Whereas in 1960 there were 0.42 hectares per capita of farmland in the world, by 2050 this figure is expected to drop to 0.19 hectares per capita.[9]

The demand for fertilizer to increase food production is growing and will continue unabated. Potassium is a necessary ingredient of fertilizer, and it comes from potash. Fifty percent of the free world's minable potash reserves are in Saskatchewan. There are potash resources in New Brunswick, and these were mined until 2015, when PCS found they could not be profitably mined, and ceased operation of its mine in that province.[10]

Potash enables growers to produce more food per land unit several times over. Potassium is also essential for human and animal growth and well-being.[11] Close to 95 percent of potash taken from the ground is used in fertilizer production, with the balance used in manufactured chemical mixtures such as detergents.[12]

Along with population growth and higher living standards, increased knowledge of the benefits of fertilization drives increased demand. People may decrease their dependence on fossil fuels, but the demand for food is here to stay.

Potash is, therefore, a very valuable commodity. The potash business has become more and more profitable in recent decades. While commodity markets, including potash, tend to be volatile, the long-term prospects for potash appear to be solid, and prices appear to be trending steadily upward.[13]

Canada is the world's largest producer and exporter of potash. It has the world's largest potash reserves, at 1 billion tonnes, enough to supply the world for many centuries. Canada produces and sells more than 30 percent of the potash used annually in the world. Russia and Belarus produce about 20 percent and 18 percent, respectively.[14]

Potash has been the second most important mineral in Canada, in terms of value of production, second only to gold.[15] The 2019 price of about US$260 per tonne amounted to about US$5 billion (more than Can$6.5 billion) in 2019. By 2022, production of potash was in the $18 billion range.[16] At that level, potash will rival gold as Canada's most important mineral. The value of gold produced from Canada was $13.7 billion in 2021.[17]

All that Canadian production of potash comes from Saskatchewan. While Saudi Arabia's oil and Alberta's natural gas may someday be replaced by other sources of energy, there is no compelling reason to find a substitute for Saskatchewan's potash, and no practical way to do so.

Saskatchewan has not only all the economically minable potash in Canada, but also the richest potash deposits in the world and the most efficient production, because of thick, relatively level, and large layers of potash ore, making it more economical to mine. The province is blessed with the best potash and the most economically extractable potash.

In addition, unlike Russia and Belarus, Saskatchewan is a stable democracy and rule of law makes it an attractive place to produce potash.

We say Canada has half the free world's potash reserves, but it would be more accurate to say that Saskatchewan has half the free world's potash reserves. Eighty percent of those reserves are owned by the 1.3 million residents of that province. It is important to understand the difference between ownership of the underground potash reserves and ownership of potash mines. The potash in the ground is owned by the province and some private owners who acquired mineral rights from the Canadian Pacific Railway, Hudson's Bay Company, or their successors.[18] Potash companies do not own the potash itself. The companies own the mines and mills, which are used to extract and refine potash ore. They have the right to access the potash by entering into a mineral lease with the potash owners, primarily the Crown, which permits them to extract potash in return for a royalty payment. In addition to having the right to a royalty payment, the Saskatchewan government can also levy taxes on the profits of the potash companies. When a potash company is sold, it is the mines and mills that are sold, along with any contractual rights under a mineral lease, not the potash reserves. Those continue to be owned by the public. When BHP made its bid to purchase PCS in 2010, it was bidding to buy its mines, mills, and mineral leases. The public's ownership of the potash reserves was not impacted.

Potash is Saskatchewan's largest export. Potash exports of $6 billion in 2020 were greater than exports of crude oil at $5 billion, and ahead of any single agricultural commodity.[19] In 2021, the value of potash sales rose to $7.6 billion[20] and was close to $18 billion in 2022.[21]

While Saskatchewan has traditionally been thought of as an agricultural power (which it is, having over 40 percent of Canada's arable land), mineral extraction is by far the province's largest industry, accounting for over 25 percent of its GDP.[22] In comparison, agriculture, forestry, fishing, and hunting combined comprise over 8 percent of the provincial economy.[23]

Saskatchewan has seen branch plant mines developed and owned by nine separate companies based outside the province; the creation of the Crown-owned Potash Corporation of Saskatchewan, which acquired five existing mines; the privatization of PCS; and later the merger of PCS with Agrium to create Nutrien. As will be detailed in chapter 8, profits have soared to new heights over the last decade and a half, with no proportionate increase to Saskatchewan's share of the profits amassed from the inherent value of the province's potash.

While the importance of potash may be largely unknown to most Canadians, it is the hottest commodity going and offers the greatest value for the world. It comes from a land that seems to have gone to sleep, as big capital has increasingly vested full control of the industry, with a steadily decreasing return to the province in distributing essentially windfall profits and the continued erosion of participation by Saskatchewan people and their government in decisions that impact the potash market and, therefore, impact the people of the province. While the people of Saskatchewan feel the impact of these decisions most directly, Canadians generally should also be concerned, given implications that arise as to whether Canadians are sufficiently involved in the stewardship of the country's natural resources. Along with the question of economic sovereignty, and return from non-renewable resources, there are implications for world food supply, which Canadians may wish to examine. In addition to wanting resource management in Canada to be profitable and sustainable, they may wish to be assured that the potash industry operates in accordance with moral and ethical standards consistent with their values. In the face of a hungry and sometimes starving world population, and the need to prevent uprisings and wars triggered by food supply issues and indifference toward the hungry, potash, like fossil fuels, raises important issues worthy of attention.

The importance of potash to Saskatchewan, and the opportunity it presents to improve quality of life in the province, cannot be overestimated. Consider that Saudi Arabia, which has approximately 226.5 billion barrels of oil in reserve, is the world's second-largest oil producer. Everyone is aware of the huge influence of Saudi Arabia through the Organization of Petroleum Exporting Countries (OPEC) on the global oil market and thereby on many aspects of economic life all around the world.[24]

Saudi Arabia's oil reserves are about 18 percent of world reserves.[25]

Saskatchewan, by contrast, has over half of the world's known potash reserves. To further put Saskatchewan's dominance in the world's potash market in perspective, consider what Norway has done with its 0.46 percent of normal oil reserves—that's less than half of 1 percent. It has leveraged its oil reserves hugely to provide its people and treasury with almost unimaginable monetary reward.

Saudi Arabia's 18 percent of world oil reserves and Norway's half-a-percent make them significant players in the world market because those nations have decided they should be the main beneficiaries of their resource wealth. Their governments have ensured the benefit from oil development accrues to the jurisdiction and its people. To say that Saskatchewan is the Saudi Arabia of potash is no exaggeration; in fact, it is an understatement.

Both Saudi Arabia and Norway decided decades ago to assume all (in the case of Saudi Arabia) and most (in the case of Norway) of the ownership and operation of oil extraction. They wanted to get the profit made from extraction of their resource into public accounts, in addition to payment of royalties and taxes.

The point here is that resource wealth can be a means to enrich the jurisdiction and its population more significantly. The resources belong to them. Their government manages resources on behalf of the public as owner. Obtaining payments truly reflecting resource value can be achieved through participating in its extraction, not simply by receiving payments in the form of royalty for the raw material and taxes on the profit, but also by directly receiving some of the profits. If public ownership is not desired, adequate revenue from resources can also be achieved by ensuring returns in the form of royalties and taxes earned on profits that reflect the true value of the resource. Just as the government can adjust tax rates for individuals, they can adjust them for potash companies. In Saudi Arabia, two-thirds of government revenue comes from the country's oil operations.[26]

In Norway, net cash from oil was estimated at NOK 184 billion in 2021, amounting to 20–30 percent of government revenue.[27] The bulk of oil revenue comes from Equinor ASA (formerly, Statoil), the state-owned oil producer. Norway's long-term policy is to ensure oil profits "benefit Norwegian society as a whole, and that future generations will benefit."[28] It is a stated goal that "exploration, development, and production must result in maximum value creation for society, and that revenues must accrue to the Norwegian state and thus benefit society as a whole."[29]

The people of Norway, and their governments, whether social democratic or conservative, opted to take 70 percent of Norwegian oil production into public hands. Equinor had assets of US$111 billion as of 2018. Norway protects its citizens who rely on government programs and services and protects the government from the ups and downs of the commodity market through its sovereign wealth fund, valued today at more than US$700 billion. In addition, both private and public sectors in Norway accrue wealth through economic diversification, which public policy ensures is connected to the extraction industry. Investment in technology has enabled Norway to produce oil in the most economically and environmentally sound manner with an above average recovery rate.[30] If Norway can do that with 0.5 percent of world oil reserves, it does not seem unreasonable to wonder what Saskatchewan might accomplish with 50 percent of the world's potash reserves.

Whatever can be said for the strong preference in North America to relinquish the business of resource extraction to private interests, the last few decades have made it clear in jurisdictions such as Saskatchewan and Alberta that huge endowments of natural resources do not suffice on their own to protect against the ups and downs of commodity markets or to provide any significant heritage funds for future generations. The fully private resource extraction model has not produced any cushioning for governments, although that has not necessarily led them to question whether it is the best approach.

Prior to oil discovery, Saudi Arabia was an impoverished nation. It acquired its oil industry through purchase, after several decades of foreign ownership of extraction infrastructure. Whatever else can be said about Saudi Arabia, no one can accuse it of being run by radical leftists. Nor can it be said that either of the states mentioned here are incompetent to manage the resource extraction industry. The prevalent North American attitude that public ownership is dangerous and radical does not prevail in other places, and they seem to do just fine.

Public ownership of all or part of resource extraction facilities can operate successfully. It is not, however, the only model that benefits the public. Private or cooperative ownership are other models and could meet the public's need as resource owner to obtain a fair return through royalties and taxes of the profits generated through mineral extraction, provided the government ensures there is a balance between what the mining companies get and what the public receives, reflecting the value of the resource provided to the companies.

BRANCH PLANT POTASH MINE DEVELOPMENT

POTASH WAS DISCOVERED IN SASKATCHEWAN IN THE 1940S WHILE oil companies were drilling for oil. The province's potash resource was seen to be rich and vast. However, it was very deep underground, with water deposits between it and the surface.

It was not known how to extract Saskatchewan potash without water flooding into the shafts and mines from the underground water deposits above. In the early 1960s, technology and methodology to freeze the ground around the shaft and to line the shaft with steel rings impervious to water (known as the Blairmore Ring) was developed. For many years, a section of the Blairmore Ring was on a pedestal in a riverbank park in Saskatoon because its development enabled a lot of economic activity. Along with freezing, the Blairmore Ring made it possible to mine potash in Saskatchewan. Given the nature of the resource, there was no shortage of companies anxious to build mines, and several went into production throughout the 1960s. Development, all by the private sector, began under the Co-operative Commonwealth Federation (CCF) government and continued after the Liberal Party was elected in 1964. The following companies developed ten mines between 1958 and 1970, and became operational in the years indicated:

- Potash Company of America (PCA) (Saskatoon), 1960
- International Minerals and Chemical Corporation (Canada) Ltd. (IMC) (Esterhazy), 1962

- Kalium Chemicals Ltd. (Belle Plaine), 1964
- IMC K2 (Esterhazy), 1967
- Texasgulf Potash (Allan), 1968
- Duval Corporation of Canada (Cory), 1968
- Alwinsal Potash of Canada Ltd. (Lanigan), 1968
- Central Canada Potash Co. Ltd. (Colonsay), 1969
- Cominco Ltd. (Vanscoy), 1969
- Hudson Bay Mining and Smelting Co. Ltd. (Rocanville), 1970

Nine multinational corporations or their subsidiaries built ten mines over the course of twelve years.[1] They brought benefits to the province, providing jobs and economic activity. Potash development was welcome in a province that historically did not attract big money. Alberta's light sweet crude oil discovered in the 1940s moved that province ahead of Saskatchewan in economic and population terms. Saskatchewan remained "next year country." The 1960s were seen as a pivotal turning point, and there was hope that Saskatchewan's day in the sun had finally arrived.

Arguably, investment came in too fast. While there was a market for potash as an important ingredient of fertilizer, by the late 1960s, the ten new mines, in addition to several mines in the United States, meant that supply exceeded demand. As with all commodities, the solution to the high cost of commodities is the high cost of commodities. As prices go up or new opportunities arise, many players rush in to get a piece of the market. This not-unusual situation was almost guaranteed by the Saskatchewan government's potash taxation and royalty policy in the 1960s. Liberal Premier Ross Thatcher was determined to grow Saskatchewan's economy. He granted potash companies who built mines in Saskatchewan lower royalties for eighteen years. To qualify for the royalty reduction, a company had to make a development decision by the end of 1967, which coincidentally was also an election year in Saskatchewan. From a practical perspective, that meant that if a mining company wanted to mine potash in Saskatchewan in the ensuing eighteen years, it had to make the decision that year. Otherwise, it couldn't compete with other producers, who would have a lower tax rate.

It can be said that Thatcher's policy had the unintended consequence of causing oversupply in the late 1960s, resulting in trouble for the companies and unemployment. However, the world potash market recovered by

1973 or 1974. As will be discussed herein, the policy of the NDP government in the early part of the twenty-first century was fairly similar. It gave tax breaks for refurbishing and expanding the industry, because the government sought more economic activity and jobs and wanted to ensure that Saskatchewan remained a world leader in potash production. That policy, like Thatcher's, kick-started huge investments in potash mines and mills in Saskatchewan, which became perhaps more influenced by world market conditions as the years went on. These policies in the 1960s and the 2000s ran the risk of overbuilding and oversupply. Probably, however, that risk was outweighed by the benefit of having the infrastructure in place, as it resulted in huge capital investments and provided the province with the ability to be a market leader for decades to come. As well, these policies provided the opportunity to make money from volume and not from high price alone. BHP's entry into the potash mining industry in Saskatchewan is another factor that will be discussed and considered in this book. As will be shown, productive capacity has increased dramatically and is planned to continue to do so into the next decade. No one knows what the future holds in terms of markets. We do know, however, that the demand for food will grow, and Saskatchewan will be very well positioned to meet that global demand.

Because all the potash mining companies prior to 1976 were part of parent companies that had many and varied interests beyond potash mining and were all headquartered outside the province, they did not have a singular focus on potash mining in Saskatchewan. Developing potash mining in Saskatchewan was very much a classic case of branch plant development. A lack of familiarity and understanding of Saskatchewan sensitivities and priorities probably played a role in breaking down the relationship between the industry and the government of Saskatchewan in the 1970s. Companies may also have had a sense of unease about the NDP government, which indicated that there should be a higher return from the sale of potash, and in its 1971 election platform promised "an NDP government would consider the feasibility of bringing the potash industry under public ownership."[2]

Maximizing shareholder value is the goal of every publicly traded corporation and the potash mining companies were no exception. Government, on the other hand, has a responsibility to maximize benefits for the public, in this case the people of Saskatchewan, as owners of the resource, and may bring other considerations to the table, such as orderly regulation of production to avoid some of the boom/bust nature of commodity markets, and provide more steady employment numbers, revenue, and increased market share for Saskatchewan.

Fast forward to 2022, and the ten mines built in the 1960s, now largely refurbished and expanded, are owned by two large corporations, Nutrien and The Mosaic Company. The process of consolidating the industry began not through corporate mergers, but through the creation of the Crown-owned PCS, which acquired mines located at Saskatoon, Allan, Cory, Lanigan, and Rocanville. Mosaic now owns the four other original mines: Esterhazy (two mines), Belle Plaine, and Colonsay. And Nutrien now owns the five mines that were acquired by PCS and the Vanscoy mine formerly owned by Agrium.

THREE

PUBLIC OWNERSHIP THROUGH THE POTASH CORPORATION OF SASKATCHEWAN

ALLAN BLAKENEY'S NDP DEFEATED THE LIBERAL GOVERNMENT OF Ross Thatcher in June of 1971. Later, upon re-election in June 1975, the NDP government would pass legislation authorizing the Government of Saskatchewan to expropriate the assets of Saskatchewan potash producers, subject to a requirement to pay fair market value as negotiated with the companies, or as determined through independent arbitration, with a right to appeal to the courts. Also in 1975, the government was preparing to establish the Potash Corporation of Saskatchewan as a Crown corporation. It would acquire and operate some potash mines through negotiations with, and the payment of fair market value to, the former owners, without exercising the expropriation power.

Some may suppose that these dramatic developments came about solely due to an ideological predilection on the social democratic NDP government's part favouring public ownership of resource companies. Certainly that was a factor, but public ownership was not a foregone conclusion. The reality was more complex, and, as with any conflict, the result of actions on both sides. The action the government took was a response to the attitudes and behaviour of the industry, as well as for ideological reasons. Of course, the industry's conduct was in response to the government's policies and uncertainty regarding the government's intentions. Nevertheless, the industry's approach represented a challenge to the government's stated objectives of obtaining a fair share of potash profits for the people of Saskatchewan and expanding production in the province. At the end of the day, the elected government had the final say.

The CCF government of 1944–1964 (the NDP's predecessor) had made a conscious decision to pursue development of the potash mining industry through the private sector,[1] so it was not necessarily the case that the government would be directly involved in potash mining. Other circumstances were at play.

The Thatcher Liberal government's policy to require potash companies to make a development decision by 1967 or face higher taxes worked well to get the mines built. It also resulted in increasing supply far beyond the demand for potash in the late 1960s. The mines were operating at less than 50 percent capacity and the price dropped by 40 percent in the late 1960s.[2] The NDP's 1971 election platform commitment to obtain a greater share of revenue from potash mining for the public treasury, combined with the companies' financial difficulty at the time, would have aggravated the industry. By 1974, however, prices had recovered and begun to rise.[3]

In 1973, the Saskatchewan NDP government conducted an analysis of potash industry revenues. The review, which did not have access to complete information about the companies' actual production costs, led the government to believe the province was not receiving an adequate share of the profits earned from potash mining. It also convinced the government that the province could have a larger share of the world market with more production. The government asked the companies for financial information to verify costs.[4] It also indicated to the industry that the government wanted public participation in new or expanded potash extraction facilities. Public participation would give the government a "window" into the industry by having first-hand knowledge of the challenges and costs involved.

With a provincial election coming the next year, in 1974, several potash companies announced they were delaying expansion plans, notwithstanding rising demand for potash.[5] Such news was not what the people of the province wanted and it contradicted the government's strong feeling that the industry should be expanded. Given that demand was growing, the industry's stance was likely intended to dampen the prospects of the government's re-election and to indicate that the industry would prefer the government be defeated after one term. Unfortunately, from the companies' point of view, that did not occur.

It cannot be assumed conflict would not have arisen had the Liberals remained in power. They may have found the industry's approach to be as objectionable as the NDP government did later. Liberal Premier Thatcher was an able, if somewhat crusty, politician who was not afraid of a fight on Saskatchewan's behalf. He died shortly after the 1971 election. It is fair to assume, however, that the Liberals would not have pursued the aggressive policies ultimately pursued under Premier Blakeney.

The history of discussions between the government and the industry is well documented elsewhere.[6] The companies' refusal to provide the government with information on the volume of potash taken out of the ground, potash which was owned by the public and for which royalties were required to be paid, as well as their refusal to provide financial information that would verify claims that they could not afford to pay more to the public treasury, were bound to increase tension with the government. In addition, the companies, which were challenging the province's taxes in court, refused to pay certain taxes that were due commencing in June 1975.[7] These actions amounted to a direct challenge to the elected government and breached provincial law.

Blakeney had assumed that once the June 1975 election was over, if the NDP was re-elected, the companies would abandon such positions and work with the government to determine how the industry would grow and the province reap more benefit. He was convinced that the companies had greater capacity to pay.[8]

Blakeney wrote: "I was very surprised when following our re-election there was not a contact from the industry indicating a desire to bargain. Instead, nine days after the election, the companies launched a legal action."[9] The companies challenged the government's tax regulations in one lawsuit, and in another, they challenged a pro-rationing scheme they had begged Premier Thatcher to agree to with the Governor of New Mexico. Potash mining also took place at that time in that US state. Pro-rationing was a scheme to deal with oversupply and low prices. It involved the assignment of market share to the various companies, some of which operated both in Canada and the United States, to keep the industry alive. Blakeney and the NDP had opposed pro-rationing. When Blakeney became premier, the companies persuaded him to leave pro-rationing in place.

Accordingly, the premier felt the court action taking the government to task for pro-rationing "was bad faith in the extreme,"[10] since it was the industry itself that had convinced a very reluctant Blakeney to continue to participate in the pro-rationing scheme.

The industry's position was that it would not expand potash mining in Saskatchewan until the government changed its policies. If the elected government's public policy was that the industry needed to expand, and if the private sector indicated they were not going to expand it, the logical result would have to be expansion through public participation in the industry. Seeing this as a possible option would certainly be reasonable since a social democratic government was in power. Whether or not the industry had considered the implications of its approach is not known. It was an approach, however, that encouraged the government to establish its approach in the very way that it did in 1974–1975.

Certainly, a government led by Blakeney would not rule out public ownership as an option. This was an environment where certain positions taken by the companies and the federal Liberal government would influence the provincial government to create a Crown corporation to mine potash because such a solution would get around the companies' lack of cooperation and a federal government budget change. Circumstances led him to conclude that the public interest would best be served through public ownership of part of the industry.

Blakeney described the considerations leading to the decision to pursue public ownership in his memoir. The government was facing challenges from the potash companies and the federal Liberal government. In 1974, federal Minister of Finance John Turner's budget did away with the longstanding ability of oil and potash companies to deduct royalty payments as expenses against income. This hampered the companies' profitability and limited the province's ability to tax such producers.

> What we were seeing was an industry lashing out against a government that they felt was abusing them. We felt that the industry was laying at our door the sins of the federal government and were declining even to enter into negotiations with us. In addition, they were withholding taxes that they fully acknowledged were due and payable. All of these events were the background for a decision that we made in August 1975 to acquire, if we could, a significant part of the potash industry of Saskatchewan.[11]

Blakeney saw several advantages to public ownership:

The first would be to place beyond the reach of the federal government the returns from that part of the potash industry that was owned by the Crown. Secondly, it would signal to Ottawa that the vehicle of public ownership was available for other industries, namely oil and uranium, if they persisted in their policy of attempting to get for themselves a substantial part of the increased value of these resources. Thirdly, it would signal to the potash industry that it was wholly unacceptable for the industry to withhold taxes that were acknowledged to be due and owing and would signal to them also that there were other options for developing the potash industry in Saskatchewan, and accordingly that they could not name their own terms. Negotiations were required. Fourthly, it would signal to other resource industries that our government considered public ownership of some of the resources as an option, and we believed that this would be part of their thinking when negotiating with the government.[12]

As well, there was a sense that public ownership would contribute to Saskatchewan being more of a master in its own house.

Finally, some of us felt that the public ownership of some resource industries would cause some in our party and other groups in the community, particularly the academic community, to consider the economic future of Saskatchewan in a different light. We hoped that we could encourage people to regard the future as not wholly determined by decisions made by foreign resource companies but to be partly determined by Saskatchewan people themselves. This is the germ of the idea that later became the 1978 election slogan, "We Can Do It Ourselves." It was, in an inchoate way, a declaration of independence from the federal government and of more independence from the international resource companies.[13]

The combined impact of the approach taken by the industry and the fact that a provincial Crown corporation was exempt from paying taxes to the federal government made it easier for the government to opt for public ownership. As well, public ownership would give the province a vehicle to secure expansion of productive capacity, and it would give the government an accurate read on the operating costs of potash mines. Blakeney saw the need to "signal" to the potash companies that they could not set their own terms. This suggests that he felt the companies did not contemplate that the government would or could get into the potash business. If that was the case, it was a miscalculation. The way events transpired suggests the companies did not understand the province's resolve. They may have felt that it was a staring contest where Blakeney would eventually have to blink first if they didn't pay taxes or provide information about potash's removal from the ground. Once PCS was formed, the government gathered first-hand knowledge of the operational costs and the companies fell into line, providing information and paying taxes. Blakeney was not about to blink. Another possible explanation is that the companies were simply waiting to see whether there would be a change of government in 1975.

In February 1975, Elwood Cowley, Saskatchewan's young and astute minister of mineral resources, announced the formation of the Potash Corporation of Saskatchewan. He cited increasing demand and a need for greater Saskatchewan participation in decisions that would influence the potash market and therefore the economy of Saskatchewan. He also spoke of the need for greater benefit for the province from development. A team of experienced experts from the private sector and the public sector was assembled to create a plan that could be used in the event it became necessary.[14]

While the industry's stated intention not to expand would have influenced the government to conclude public participation was necessary, the industry's refusal to provide information the government requested to verify production costs and profit levels would similarly influence the government. If the information was not provided, the only way the government would know what the costs actually were would be by having a direct stake in the industry.

The Blakeney government felt it was being pushed into a corner by the companies, by court rulings resulting from some of the companies' legal challenges to government taxation, and by the federal government in Ottawa. The federal budget change was yet another development that encouraged public involvement in potash mining. A Crown corporation operating a potash mine, in addition to being a means of expanding the industry, would avoid the problem of non-deductibility of royalty payments, since the federal government cannot tax provincial governments or provincial Crown corporations.

Blakeney, like Premier Thatcher, was no fool. A Rhodes Scholar, he was legally trained and had held senior positions in the CCF governments of Saskatchewan in the 1950s. He was a brilliant administrator, analyst, and strategist and a respected political leader. On November 12, 1975, the recently re-elected NDP government provided its Speech from the Throne to Lieutenant Governor Dr. Stephen Worobetz to deliver to the Legislative Assembly. The speech referred to "the right of the people of Saskatchewan to receive their fair share of benefits from the development of their resources,"[15] including revenues, jobs, and conservation, and "achieving greater control over their own destiny."[16]

The Speech from the Throne reflected the government's view that it would not meet the priorities of making Saskatchewan a larger player in the world potash market and obtaining a greater return for the public if production was left solely in the hands of the private potash companies.

The industry's unhappiness was and remains understandable. They had made substantial investments. They had gone through a market downturn. The government could pass legislation to maneuver around some court rulings, and the NDP wanted more return from the companies.

As is detailed in chapter 8 and appendix A, when Blakeney assumed office in 1971, the government's share of potash profits, measured as a percentage of the government's estimate of the value of potash sales for the year, amounted to 1.91 percent. By 1974, it was 11.10 percent.

Another factor, as Blakeney recounted, that led to the government arriving at its policy position was an unwillingness to cave in to demands by companies who were disobeying valid regulations requiring information to be provided and who were refusing to pay some taxes as they fell due. This was in addition to thwarting the public policy objective of building a stronger industry in Saskatchewan. In a democracy, everyone must obey the law and pay their taxes, and public policy is determined by the elected government. Pressure tactics which flout the law used to impose the will of a particular group, certainly including foreign multinationals, undermine the basic rules of a healthy democracy. It is no surprise that such approaches were found not to be acceptable.

On November 12, 1975, Lieutenant Governor Worobetz carried out his public duty of reading the Speech from the Throne written by the provincial government. The speech recited what had occurred in discussions between government and industry and the options the government felt it had. The Lieutenant Governor stated:

> My Government has attempted to work out an accommodation with these companies which would—through regulation, taxation and participation in their future expansion—guarantee greater production capacity, and an assured fair return to the Province and a greater ownership role for the people of Saskatchewan.
>
> My Government has been frustrated in these attempts.
>
> The response of a majority of the companies has been to decline to provide information required to be provided by law, to decline to proceed with expansion required to meet anticipated future demand and to challenge in a series of legal actions the right of the Province of Saskatchewan to conserve the resource and to collect taxes from the industry.
>
> My Government has given careful consideration to its stated objectives of ensuring expansion of potash production and an assured fair return and a greater participating role for the people of Saskatchewan and has concluded that these are valid and vital objectives to be pursued.[17]

The speech stated the government faced three options. The first option was to retreat and accommodate its policies to industry willingness to comply and, from its point of view, "surrender for future generations of Saskatchewan people their heritage from this vast resource."[18]

The second option was to stand still, permit uncertainties to continue, and through delay, risk losing its position in the world potash market and future tax revenue. Inaction could also require the government to comply with court decisions that it refund hundreds of millions of dollars in taxes.

The third option was to regain provincial control of the potash resource by taking decisive action, including legislation, to enable government to acquire the assets of some or all of the producing potash mines in the province.[19] If the government had failed up to that point to alert the industry that it was determined in its approach, surely that would have reinforced the message. If not, the speech went on to say that negotiations to reach agreements with the companies for the sale of mines would be possible, in which case the legislation authorizing the government to expropriate would not be necessary, but that the government was prepared to expropriate assets if necessary. In such cases the fair market value would be paid as agreed to or as determined by an impartial board of arbitration, the decision of which could be appealed in the courts.

The creation of its own potash company, the government said through the speech, would pay for itself without new taxes or diverting existing government revenue. Jobs would be preserved, and new ones created. The province's ability (through the government) to ensure orderly expansion of production for future market needs would be assured, for the overall stabilization of the industry, and a secure flow of revenue for the province. As well, it was stated there would be additional research activities in the province, and the presence of senior management decision-makers, with the head office in Saskatchewan.[20]

An examination of the finances of potash mining over the years since 1995, as detailed in chapter 8, would make it difficult to argue with the government's statement the mines could pay for themselves. The only question, especially in the case of PCS, would be how many times over.

The government conveyed the message in the speech that it was prepared to be flexible and was willing to enter into joint ventures or other arrangements as long as the objective of maximizing public benefit was met. It conveyed its orientation by saying that while economic development was important, there were limits to "loss of revenue and loss of local control"[21] that were acceptable. The government was not in favour of private investment at any cost. The speech outlined the government's plan to work with various resource industries to ensure some Saskatchewan participation. This was said to be especially important in the case of potash, which it stated was "perhaps our most important non-renewable resource,"[22] noting that it was one of the largest reserves in the world. The importance of potash to global food production was also noted.

On November 18, 1975, Saskatchewan Attorney General Roy Romanow, a future premier of the province, introduced Bill No. 1, *An Act Respecting the Development of Potash Resources in Saskatchewan*. He said the Act would be seen in the future as having ushered in "a new era in resource management for Saskatchewan and for Canada."[23] The government clearly had high hopes, since the approach of the bill was not consistent with resource development in Canada or North America generally. It was quite different.

Romanow stated that for most resource industries in Saskatchewan, the government had been able to deal with the companies involved to achieve what it considered to be development representing an appropriate balance between private profit and public benefit. He stated "this approach does not work when it comes to the large potash multinational corporations."[24] Romanow claimed the province had been put in a corner by the actions of the potash companies and "challenged at almost every turn....Some might even say that the large international magnates in charge of the potash development in this province have tried to paralyze the government's resource policy." He continued: "Paralyze it why? Because we had the temerity to claim that we could make the potash companies pay a little more extra taxes for the exploitation of our potash resources."[25]

Anyone who knew Allan Blakeney or knows Roy Romanow will be aware they were anything but reckless decision-makers, and came to conclusions only after exhaustive consideration, consultation, and deliberation. It seemed clear the government felt the industry was not respectful of the provincial government's prerogative to determine resource development policy, and action was required to protect the public interest, even if it was controversial.

The creation of PCS as a Crown corporation made it clear that Blakeney and his colleagues in government were people who acted out of principle—as they saw it—and stood their ground. They undoubtedly hoped that the vision they achieved, and which took hold in Saskatchewan for a decade and a half in the twentieth century, would capture the imagination and support of a broad range of people and would be sustained. This had been the experience a little more than a decade before, when the province introduced medicare, which was very controversial, but, by the early 1970s had been adopted across Canada and today is viewed by Canadians as an important part of Canadian citizenship. They were not dreamers of small dreams. They hoped they could once again successfully go against conventional wisdom and show that things could be done just as well, or better, in a different way.

Ultimately, it could be said they failed. Their vision was implemented but undone. However, it could also be said they serve as a good example of courage of conviction. They assembled a corporation large enough to influence the world market and that served as the foundation of something even larger. They established head office presence and hundreds of white-collar jobs in Saskatchewan. For a time, Saskatchewan had real influence over the world market. People can debate the philosophical merits of their approach, or the companies' approach; still, no one can deny that they did accomplish big things. Readers can look at the profits of potash and decide for themselves whether the alternate vision achieved by successive governments has served the province well since 1989.

The NDP government made it clear that regardless of its less than warm relationship with the potash companies, the Potash Corporation of Saskatchewan would acquire assets through negotiation, if possible, and fair market value would be paid. If the parties could not agree, and the government expropriated a mine, the company concerned could take the matter to arbitration. If still dissatisfied, the company could appeal the valuation to the courts. The process gave the same protection as would be the case if a municipality expropriated a person's land for a public purpose and then some, in the sense that the companies would have three kicks at the can: negotiation, arbitration, and litigation. Citizens whose property is expropriated do not receive the arbitration option.

Creation of the world's largest potash producer occurred remarkably quickly and went fairly smoothly. "Most of the 14 companies operating in Saskatchewan at that time were large, diversified multinational corporations for whom the potash component of their holdings was relatively minor."[26] Although they opposed the government's policies, their overall interests were not at risk.

The government paid fair market value, possibly overly generous amounts, according to economist John Richards. High debt charges affected the rate of return, but not so much that PCS was not profitable.[27]

The first mine purchased was Duval Corporation's Cory mine, just west of Saskatoon. Duval was a wholly owned subsidiary of Pennzoil, whose president described the negotiations as occurring in an "amicable, highly professional businesslike way."[28] Between 1976 and 1978, PCS acquired four mines completely and 60 percent of a fifth mine.

PCS as a Crown corporation operated successfully. A study for the Economic Council of Canada by Dr. Nancy Olewiler, a resource economist at Queen's University, found that for the years 1979 to 1981, the investment yielded an after-tax return of 21 percent, 34 percent, and 26 percent. She noted the returns "added large sums to the provincial revenues well beyond what the mines PCS purchased would have generated through provincial taxes if they had remained in the private sector."[29] The study compared the performance of PCS with the performance of the private potash companies in the initial years. It found that for the years 1979 to 1984, PCS had an average profit margin of 18.2 percent per year while the combined average for the private companies was 11.43 percent per year.[30]

Critics' assertion that Allan Blakeney and his mineral resources minister Elwood Cowley did not know how to mine potash was correct. Just like other owners, however, they knew how to hire people who did.

The government initially acquired 40 percent of the industry.[31] The province had created a major world player in the potash sector, controlled and headquartered in Saskatchewan, with its head office in Saskatoon. During the initial fifteen years of potash mining in Saskatchewan, no single producer was big enough to influence the world potash market. The creation of PCS as a Crown corporation in 1975 represented the first conglomeration of potash production into one giant company. This conglomeration enabled Saskatchewan to have a direct influence on the world market through decisions made within the province. As well, government ownership meant the market could be influenced, taking Saskatchewan's interests into account. PCS adopted a plan to become a world-scale fertilizer manufacturer and seek reasonable returns but not necessarily the highest price possible. It was determined that, in the long run, the plan would meet a responsibility "to all people in the world" and would allow developing countries to afford potash.[32] The policy favoured profit from high volume rather than high prices. PCS wanted a larger market share than Canadian Potash Exporters (Canpotex) permitted, so PCS resolved in 1981 to exit Canpotex (the marketing cartel for offshore potash sales on behalf of Saskatchewan potash producers) and do its own marketing. That plan was reversed after the NDP government was defeated in the 1982 election.[33]

As long as PCS operated as a robust player in the market, the people of the province were not spectators awaiting corporate expansion and supply decisions made elsewhere, where the decisions were less impactful. The province was a decision-maker and a market player, and could produce potash, taking the interests of the province into account, and work to maintain the dominant role Saskatchewan had taken in the industry.

One of the intended moves of PCS was to depart from Canpotex. PCS initially intended to create its own marketing arm. Canpotex operated based on one vote per company. PCS had 40 percent of the industry. It was outvoted by smaller producers which also had one vote each, and would not allow PCS a share of the market commensurate with the fact that it had acquired the mines of several companies and produced by far the largest amount of potash.[34] Ultimately, this goal would be abandoned after the government changed in 1982 and did not serve to strengthen the performance of PCS during the difficult years in the 1980s. PCS acquired the Allan (initially 60 percent), Cory, Lanigan, Rocanville, and Saskatoon mines. Private operators continued to operate other mines, namely International Minerals and Chemical Corporation (Canada) at Esterhazy (K1 and K2 mines, now Mosaic mines), Kalium Chemicals at Belle Plaine (now Mosaic), Central Canada Potash at Colonsay (now Mosaic), and Cominco at Vanscoy. The Vanscoy mine was owned and operated by Cominco from its development, and eventually operated by Agrium, a division of Cominco spun off to run fertilizer operations. Agrium merged with PCS effective January 1, 2018, to create Nutrien.

The early days of PCS were prosperous, and PCS was a major player in the world market.[35] On an equity investment of about $420 million, it made profits of $78 million in 1979 and $167 million in 1980.[36]

Blakeney noted in his memoir that the government had no intention to purchase assets other than at fair market value, and the legislation assured that.[37]

In addition to PCS prospering, the private companies provided legally required information and paid their taxes. They continued to operate profitably.

Through PCS, government had a window into the industry and confirmed its assessment that the operators were well able to pay Saskatchewan taxes and make very satisfactory profits.[38]

Even the most ardent opponents of public enterprise had a pretty hard time failing to acknowledge that PCS was profitable.

In a paper they wrote for the conservative think tank Frontier Centre for Public Policy, Mark Moore and Aidan Vining proceeded from the assumption that profit-driven private enterprise will always perform more efficiently than public enterprise.[39] That generalization is questionable, and no proof is offered for it. While it should be acknowledged that government must consider political factors in the treatment of employees or the speed of change concerning things like rationalization, or relocation of operations, necessary change must eventually come. As well, there are demonstrated cases where public administration is more efficient than the private sector. One example is in health care, where the administrative costs of Canada's single-payer public system are far lower than in the profit-driven US model, while achieving better health outcomes. This has been well documented by the Romanow Commission on the Future of Health Care in Canada[40] and in many studies.[41] Examples could be cited of efficiently run public enterprises of various sorts. Saudi Arabia and Norway are able to operate resource extraction companies, and there is no reason why Saskatchewan cannot do the same. It involves hiring good managers and advisers.

The Saskatchewan government did so in the case of PCS. The authors of the Frontier Centre study reviewed other studies on privatization, including some that examined the privatization of PCS. Moore and Vining wrote that privatization increases efficiency and profits over time, and state that it takes many years to achieve. In comparing PCS's financial performance as a Crown corporation versus as a private company, they selected a four-year period (1984–88), years of severely depressed times for all potash producers, to assess the profitability of PCS as a Crown corporation. They left out 1976 to 1983, which were more profitable years.

For PCS as a private publicly traded company, the authors selected the twenty-one-year period of 1990–2011. It seems odd to compare four selected depressed market years to twenty-one years of slow but accelerating growth in the potash market after the privatization of PCS. That is, it seems odd to review a twenty-one-year period for the private PCS, but not include the approximate thirteen-year history of PCS as a Crown corporation. The years selected to look at PCS as a Crown corporation were years that were bad for all potash companies. On this strange basis, the authors conclude that privatization increases efficiency and profits over time, but even on that basis only after many years.

The authors state the data for the pre-privatization years prior to 1984 was incomplete. How the data was incomplete, in the case of a government company, which is subject to public accounting expectations, is not stated.

Rather than include the years in question and caveat any conclusion with a note indicating what exactly the problem with the data might be, the majority of the years of PCS operation under government control was simply excluded.

The authors do not refer to the Olewiler study, which had managed to locate financial results for the years in question. It wouldn't have been hard to find Olewiler, since she was by then also associated with Simon

Fraser University. She probably would've been happy to provide a copy of her ninety-eight-page detailed and comprehensive report on PCS performance, although a more selective approach did make the Frontier Centre's thirty-page report a quicker read.

Olewiler indicated, with respect to the years the Frontier Centre included for PCS as a Crown corporation, that it was a period of world recession, reduced planting, high interest rates, oversupply, and that 1982 and 1983 were "disastrous years."[42]

Olewiler concluded, regarding the performance of PCS compared to private producers, that the Crown corporation "did quite well for the period 1979–1982."[43] She compared the performance of the Crown corporation against that of private companies for the same period.

The authors of the Frontier Centre study themselves state:

Lack of complete data for the pre-privatization period may bias the results, as PCS as a SOE (state owned enterprise) appeared to have enjoyed considerable success during the 1977–1981 period before the potash price fell precipitously due to a strong contraction in American agriculture. In particular, after a slump in the potash market in the late 1960s, the market recovered in late 1973. US potash consumption increased at an average annual rate of 6.3 percent between 1975 and 1981. However, this period was followed by another price slump in late 1981. The 1986 price was half of the 1981 peak, largely due to the American farm policy of reducing acreage, combined with a major drought. From 1983–1985, US potash consumption declined on average by 2.5 percent per year.[44]

The most disastrous years were the ones the Frontier Centre selected to assess the performance of PCS as a Crown corporation. The authors go on to discuss the fact that after privatization, the potash market recovered, leading to a "surge in potash prices after 2007."[45] Years of growth due to improved world market conditions were used in assessing the performance of PCS as a private company.

PCS was privatized at the bottom of the market and priced accordingly. After privatization, as shall be discussed below, its market cap multiplied throughout the years. The Frontier Centre authors go on to say their methodology "clearly skews the results."[46] Therefore, they removed the years after 2007, and compared four disastrous years to eighteen years of improved profitability in order to illustrate the privatized company was more successful.[47]

Statistics can be misleading if assembled and interpreted selectively. For example, for several years, my seatmate in the Legislative Assembly of Saskatchewan was John Nilson, who is about six feet five inches. I am five feet seven inches. On occasion, when confronted by statistics being thrown around, I would say that, on average, John and I were six feet tall. It didn't make me six feet tall, even if I was, statistically.

The authors found that PCS as a privatized company achieved good results. Since there is no reason to suppose that PCS as a Crown corporation would not have achieved good results, or maybe better, the fact that PCS profited once privatized does not establish that it did well because it was privatized.

We are told, however, that from the point of view of Saskatchewan people, it doesn't really matter if PCS as a private company was more successful. The authors say increased profitability might not be any benefit to Saskatchewan people. Rather, "all the productivity and profitability measures show significant improvement after privatization. However, it is less clear whether the benefits of these improvements resulted in any gains for the residents of Saskatchewan."[48]

So, while profits went up, not necessarily due to privatization, and very likely due simply to improving world market conditions, the authors say private owners would benefit, not necessarily the people of Saskatchewan. Olewiler's study concluded, "PCS has, on average, generated positive net benefits for the residents of Saskatchewan. Because PCS generated profits for the government, revenues were higher than they would otherwise be, representing net benefit for the residents of Saskatchewan."[49] Olewiler concluded that PCS had done very well financially from its creation until 1982. In her view, creating PCS was a good investment.[50]

The Frontier Centre authors' point that any gains from privatization would not clearly accrue to the people of Saskatchewan was the same point Blakeney and Olewiler made in pointing out that there were net benefits to the Crown corporation. That was the objective of having the government involved in owning part of the industry. Moore and Vining not only didn't contradict the finding of Olewiler's study that the public fared better under government ownership than private ownership, but also suggested it as the likely result. This is from an organization dedicated to demonstrating the opposite, and which appears to have conducted its study to reflect other than favourably on PCS's performance in government hands.

If shareholders reside outside the province, and if a publicly traded company must maximize shareholder return, is that not the only logical result? How could it be otherwise? Even if the trickle-down theory of economics was valid, the profits flowing ultimately to shareholders would not trickle down to Saskatchewan people, but to people in other places. The allure of privatization in such circumstances is not easy to understand.

Success or failure of resource companies with a modicum of competent management depends upon world market conditions, not whether they are privately or publicly owned. Olewiler found that PCS performed well compared to the private companies over the same time period in identical market conditions. The Frontier Centre offers no evidence to the contrary. We could adopt an assumption that public ownership does not mean inefficiency and that Saskatchewan can operate potash extraction facilities as well as Norway and Saudi Arabia, and as well as corporate executives in Chicago for that matter. There is no evidence justifying an assumption that the private model serves the public better than the public model. In fact, the reverse might be demonstrated in some cases.

As a Crown corporation, PCS began the process of expansion and diversification. PCS's growth was central to the government's objective of expanding capacity. It would involve expanding productive capacity and, of necessity, creating a marketing system throughout North America. Canpotex conducted offshore marketing on behalf of all Canadian potash producers at the time, with the exception of marketing to the United States. Canpotex could not market potash there because it would run afoul of US antitrust laws. The United States market is the largest market for Saskatchewan potash. So, bringing together assets from five companies required the creation of a large marketing arm. For that reason, PCS established a subsidiary for marketing and distribution throughout North America, and in particular in the United States.

As well, PCS aimed to expand productive capacity and sales. Acquiring 40 percent of the potash mining industry created, for the first time, a world-scale potash producer in Saskatchewan. This made PCS the largest producer outside of the Soviet Union and East Germany.[51] A potash producer with its head office in Saskatchewan was also a first. It was decided to establish the marketing headquarters for the United States in Atlanta, Georgia.[52]

At the time PCS was created, two-thirds of Saskatchewan potash was shipped to the United States.[53] An additional subsidiary was established to oversee transportation and storage facilities.[54]

The corporation was intended to be a vehicle for Saskatchewan to influence the world potash market. John Burton stated: "A five-year plan adopted in 1978 emphasized '…it is vital PCS, in the absence of pro-rationing, establish itself as a price and product leader and in effect speak for the Saskatchewan industry.'"[55] As previously discussed, the approach was to keep volume high and make profit from high volume rather than high price. Several advantages were seen to this approach. First, it was good because it would put more people to work in Saskatchewan. Second, it was seen as a responsible plan in a world needing to be fed. Third, a high price for potash could enable competitors to enter the market. If the price was lower, since existing producers had already paid for the mining infrastructure, it was difficult for others to spend the capital required to build a greenfield (i.e., not previously developed) potash mine. Existing mining companies could more economically use the infrastructure they had to expand productive capacity.

PCS planned to bring about new production by expanding existing mines. It aimed to have 50 percent of Saskatchewan's productive capacity by the end of the 1980s and about 60 percent by 1990.[56] PCS was also exploring the possibility of diversifying into the manufacture of fertilizer.[57]

Canpotex was a major impediment to PCS expanding offshore sales, due to its previously mentioned voting structure. The smaller producers, which continued to exist, could outvote PCS. Therefore, although PCS owned 40 percent of the productive capacity, its share of the offshore market was limited to its existing allocation. Canpotex policies did not serve PCS well, and PCS resolved to exit Canpotex in 1982. A subsidiary to manage offshore marketing was created.[58]

PCS operated successfully and profitably in its first five years. It planned to invest $2.5 billion by 1990 to triple its productive capacity. The defeat of Blakeney's NDP government on April 26, 1982, brought to power a party that was not in favour of government enterprise in general and opposed to the creation of PCS in particular. The Progressive Conservative government of Grant Devine sent a message through its transition team to

PCS management even before it was sworn into office. The message was a direction to cancel plans to withdraw from Canpotex. Of course, at that point, there was no legal authority for the direction. That, however, would change very soon.[59]

The Olewiler study states: "Although PCS had over 40 percent of the productive capacity, it had only a one-seventh say in all matters."[60] The Olewiler study pointed out that during the potash market downturn of the early 1980s, production at PCS was reduced by 34 percent while the rest of the industry (i.e., the private sector) had a reduction of 23 percent. "From 1982–1983, both PCS and the private firms increased output. But the increase in PCS output was about 8 percent and for the private companies was 16 percent."[61] Maintaining PCS in Canpotex placed it at the mercy of its competitors.

To expand productive capacity, PCS planned to expand the Lanigan potash mine. Without doing its own marketing offshore and increasing its share of the market, any such expansion would prove to be an expensive and unprofitable undertaking. John Burton asserts the inability to aggressively pursue more offshore sales through PCS, combined with the new provincial government's insistence to carry on expanding the Lanigan mine and the dividend demands from the government that the corporation could not afford to pay, was devastating for the corporation. He states: "PCS was simply ground down into an emaciated skeleton clinging to the government for life-support, in stark contrast to the economic giant that was emerging only a few short years previously."[62] Leaving PCS under the thumb of its competitors at Canpotex was effectively a stranglehold on PCS in the offshore market. Yet the government would not allow PCS to delay the planned expansion at the Lanigan mine intended to meet increased market share. The premature expansion of the Lanigan mine under those circumstances cost PCS about $95 million in interest on the capital cost.[63]

Burton asserts the above directives and other directives from the government prevented PCS from operating as a commercial entity, and forced it to operate at a loss and to sell some assets at fire sale prices to other potash producers.[64] That view appears to be supported by a Peat Marwick report that noted the government had provided no clear mandate to PCS that would enable the company to arrive at a strategy. The government's political directives, Peat Marwick said, made it clear that a mission statement was needed to "state clearly whether the corporation is to act commercially or whether its role is also to meet social objectives."[65]

Notwithstanding all of the above, PCS returned to profitability prior to privatization.[66]

FOUR

PRIVATIZATION OF THE POTASH CORPORATION OF SASKATCHEWAN

THE MASSIVE DEFEAT OF ALLAN BLAKENEY'S NDP GOVERNMENT BY Grant Devine's Progressive Conservatives in the April 1982 Saskatchewan provincial election made the future of PCS as a Crown corporation uncertain, perhaps doubtful, given that it was in the hands of people opposed to its creation. Its existence as a Crown corporation would last another seven years.

The PC government was committed to a program of privatization. While it is perhaps no surprise that a conservative government would view potash mining as something the public sector should not be engaged in, it is still surprising that, from a business perspective, it would not realize that selling in a depressed market was not a good idea. As well, the implicit view that privatization would result in economic activity as money was released into the market economy (an underpinning of privatization theory) isn't going to work very well when the owners are overwhelmingly going to be out of province, and the money will not be released into the Saskatchewan economy. It is surprising these flaws in the privatization approach did not seem to dampen the enthusiasm of the Saskatchewan government.

The Devine government's ideological position was that if business was in the hands of the private sector, the economy would be more robust, as the money circulated around or trickled down to the folks at the bottom. The government may not have recognized that profits may go to shareholders outside the province, thereby theoretically circulating and trickling down where those shareholders are located, a reality recognized even by the Frontier Centre for Public Policy. Shares in the privatized PCS were sold to a variety of large investment firms and banks, and PCS no longer existed as a publicly owned company. The investment bankers undoubtedly saw an opportunity for money to be made as potash markets improved. The bulk of the money, however, would not be made in Saskatchewan.

If the vision of Blakeney, Romanow, Cowley, and others, which took Saskatchewan down a road less travelled, could have captured the hearts and minds of the people of Saskatchewan, if the extraordinary gains PCS's private owners achieved had not gone outside the province, the Saskatchewan people would have benefitted enormously. It is no great comfort to Saskatchewan people that great benefits flow to shareholders outside the province. Even the proponents of privatization say the benefit to Saskatchewan people "is quite small."[1]

Nancy Olewiler recognized this. She concluded the government's window into the industry resolved tax disputes because the government knew the cost of production. The province's return from the Crown corporation was "substantially above" what taxation of private companies would have paid.[2]

The prevailing narrative, however, was that private ownership is more efficient and profitable than public ownership, and an elected government in favour of privatization had the authority to act in accordance with that view.

PCS had done well. A 1996 analysis summarized its financial performance:

> When the Tories came to power in 1982, PCS had reported $414 million in profits with a book value of $963 million. The province held an equity position of $732 million and had a long-term debt of only $88 million. Between 1976 and 1988 it paid royalties and taxes to the provincial government totalling $372 million and paid a dividend to the province of $228 million.[3]

PCS would be an attractive asset to private investors. It had fully assembled the largest potash company in the world, mining the best and largest potash resource body in the world, in one of the best places in the world to be in business. This could especially be an attractive target during a decade when the potash industry was in a prolonged downturn, and all potash producers were either losing money or making a small profit. It might be a good time to buy, although not necessarily a good time to sell, if markets were going to recover.

PCS was the only major North American fertilizer company that remained profitable during the market downturn of the late 1980s and early 1990s.[4]

While many may assume PCS was not a money-maker, various written accounts of its history confirm it was well-run and profitable as a Crown corporation.[5]

In its first five years of operation, PCS made a profit of $413 million after paying approximately $520 million for its five mines acquired between 1976 and 1978. In addition, it paid $270 million in taxes and royalties to the province.[6]

In 1989, a public corporation, which included mining assets with a replacement cost in the billions of dollars, was sold by the Saskatchewan government for approximately $630 million. Eight years later, in 1997, its market cap was US$4.5 billion, or Can$6.2 billion—close to a tenfold increase in value.[7] That's a remarkable return on investment, which would have been realized by all the other potash companies, which held onto their assets.

In 2010, twenty-one years after privatization, BHP offered US$38.6 billion (about Can$40 billion at the time) in a hostile takeover bid for PCS. That is about forty-three times as much as PCS was sold for in 1989 in real dollar terms.

PCS was able to pay off its debt in six years after privatization.[8] In its first ten years of operation as a private company, it built upon the asset acquired from the Saskatchewan government, continuing a policy of diversification into enterprises, such as phosphate mines and nitrogen plants, and additional potash productive capacity as sales rose.[9]

Erin Weir, then an economist working for the United Steelworkers union, estimated that, as of 2011, some twenty-two years after privatization, the loss to the people of Saskatchewan in foregone revenue was between $18 billion and $36 billion.[10] That is a staggering amount for a province of about 1.3 million people. It seems unbelievable. Weir is looking at all profits PCS earned as a private corporation, not just profits from potash operations, as this book does. Weir's approach is not unreasonable; PCS could have been just as diversified as a Crown corporation as it continued to become over the years as a privately owned company. In fact, it was underway. This book takes a very conservative approach and looks only at profits derived from potash by PCS and other potash companies. It is not unreasonable, however, to consider, as Weir does, the complete profitability of PCS. As the numbers presented in chapter 8 (taken from the companies' own documents) show, the profits from potash mining are huge. Most of PCS's profit came from potash and, as the numbers in chapter 8 indicate, the profits Weir estimated are realistic.

Weir argues the 1989 sale of PCS "was the worst fiscal decision in the province's history."[11] He points out the mines sold in 1989 still accounted for more than half of PCS's profits in 2011. PCS as a private company was built upon a large platform the people of Saskatchewan put together. As former President and CEO of PCS Bill Doyle put it: "When you look at the percentage of our gross margin as a total company, the majority come from potash and we're proud to be PotashCorp."[12]

Even if we take a more conservative approach than Weir does, we still arrive at a position where the losses are very large. Those in favour of privatizing PCS, including many in Saskatchewan's business community, argue that Blakeney's creation of the corporation, coupled with the unused expropriation power, frightened business away from Saskatchewan. In reality, capital will go where it can make a reasonable rate of return. That's how capital operates.

It is important, as well, to remember that if Blakeney had not stood up to the potash producers, it would mean that government could be overruled through bad behaviour by powerful corporate interests. Saskatchewan would have suffered immensely in terms of its position as a democratic self-governing jurisdiction. As well, the mines were all branch plants; there was no potash corporate office presence in Saskatchewan prior to the creation of PCS. As a Crown corporation, PCS had its operating headquarters in Saskatoon. For many years, there was no doubt that PCS's head office was in Saskatchewan.

Saskatchewan people may have different points of view on various subjects, but one thing they would agree on is that they want to be proud of who they are and where they are. They want head offices of companies to be in Saskatchewan, where their business derives its success. They want good jobs in the province. This is especially true in the case of resource companies where the resource belongs to the public. They have the right to feel that if they are good enough to permit the extraction of the resource, they should be good enough for corporate executives to want to live among them. They don't want to be thought of as Hicksville, Nowhere. So the fact that a large corporate head office such as PCS was in Saskatchewan was important to the Saskatchewan people, as is the head office of Cameco, a uranium giant. Probably the fact that PCS was brought together and created by the Saskatchewan people, and that Cameco is an amalgam of a federal Crown corporation, Eldorado Resources, and assets of the Saskatchewan Mining Development Corporation, a provincial Crown corporation, underscores the feeling that Saskatchewan deserves major corporate presence. That includes head office jobs involving decision-makers and, where possible, value-added industry, not just provision of raw resources. In 2010, business writers in *The Globe and Mail* noted that as PCS's "financial fortunes improved, the company began a slow retreat from Saskatchewan. Citing his wife's concerns about local schools, Mr. Doyle sold the family's sprawling riverfront home in Saskatoon to move to a suburb of Chicago in 2002. Many executive office functions followed him."[13]

As industry and resources minister for Saskatchewan in the early 2000s, I was angry that Cameco decided to place some value-added industry outside Saskatchewan, which management had indicated would be located here, and I made that clear to Cameco executives. They had asked me to make it an explicit part of the NDP government's economic policy that the province would welcome some value-added processing activity, including that which they were proposing. I agreed with that, and I sought and obtained caucus and cabinet approval to do so. One morning I was parking at a shopping centre in Saskatoon and one of them, who was also a friendly acquaintance, was parking as well. I expressed my displeasure about the decision not to locate in Saskatchewan after I had proceeded to facilitate it at their request. He replied: "Well, a decision like that is the prerogative of the board of directors."

I knew that already, actually. I replied: "Yes, that's right, and a decision on the rate of taxation or royalties to be paid by resource companies is the prerogative of the government of Saskatchewan." I was subsequently told that Cameco's senior management was offended by what I said because it was a "threat."

Maybe it was a threat. If it was, I never followed through on it. The point is that if resource companies want favourable treatment from government, they should be sensitive to the aspirations of the local population and their government. One of those aspirations is to be not simply a provider of raw materials. Government should not take a hands-off approach. It should pursue maximum return for the people of the province in terms of revenue and economic development in return for extracting the province's resources.

In addition to giving the province market influence, profit, and potentially much more, PCS as a Crown corporation gave Saskatchewan people pride in their province. When PCS was privatized, they were assured the head office would remain in Saskatchewan.

When PCS was privatized in 1989, the government bill included a provision that the head office must remain in Saskatchewan, the company be majority Canadian-owned, and no more than 5 percent could be held by a single individual or company.

The head office provision was almost meaningless, because all you really have to do is designate a certain place as your head office, and that will suffice legally, whether the decisions are actually made there or not. The other restrictive provisions were removed by Romanow's NDP government in the early 1990s, at PCS's request.

Once you decide a corporation is private, it doesn't make sense to hamstring it in the marketplace or make it difficult for it to raise capital or to trade in shares. If it must adhere to rules its competitors don't have to, it creates a competitive disadvantage. Although the NDP was opposed to privatizing PCS, once PCS was private, it was not the goal of the Romanow government elected after the privatization to make it difficult for the private company to operate as such. PCS needed to be able to raise capital in the same manner as other private companies could. The restrictions on foreign ownership and maximum amount of ownership, as well intentioned as they were, may have been useful to reassure the public at the time of privatization, but if companies need capital and have trouble getting it, provisions are not serving anyone's interest.

A private corporation must be able to act accordingly. Provisions that are intended to win the public over and are not consistent with a company's ability to operate on a level playing field in the private sector are more of a public relations exercise than anything else because they usually cannot be maintained. Once a Crown corporation is gone, it's gone; in most cases, the guarantees about provincial involvement will gradually fall off as well.

Private resource companies can still be respectful of local sentiments and interests, such as the head office location. In PCS's case, it clearly needed to have officers and personnel all over North America, since it diversified operations across the continent, and no one would suggest otherwise. That doesn't mean, however, that the head office couldn't be in Saskatchewan. As a result of hollowing out the Saskatoon head office and moving the key decision-makers to its Chicago area office, by the time BHP made its hostile takeover bid for PCS in 2010, six of nine senior executives were located in Chicago, along with CEO Bill Doyle.

After PCS convinced the Saskatchewan government to oppose BHP's attempted $38.4 billion takeover, one of the conditions Brad Wall's Saskatchewan Party government extracted was that PCS would move several key executives back to Saskatoon, and Bill Doyle would acquire a residence in Saskatoon. Bill committed to becoming a Saskatoon resident and taxpayer, and claimed as his home a Saskatoon condominium that would sell for $300,000 to $325,000. The fact that PCS already owned the condo was a pretty good hint that this wasn't a likely scenario for a man with a net worth in the hundreds of millions. Doyle's move to Saskatoon even attracted the attention of the *Globe and Mail*. It reported:

Bill Doyle is going down market....[He] has become a property owner in the province again as part of the company's so-called 'Pledge to Saskatchewan,' made during its defence against BHP Billiton Ltd.'s hostile takeover bid. But this time, there is no mansion along the South Saskatchewan River for Mr. Doyle, who is one of Canada's wealthiest CEOs.

Instead, he has opted for a 1,000-square-foot condo in a 27-year-old building in Saskatoon, which he bought days after BHP's $38.6-billion deal was turned away by the federal government. The estimated value of the property: $308,000, according to the city's land titles registry.

The transaction allowed the Chicago native to stand before Saskatoon's chamber of commerce last week and proclaim himself a citizen of the city.[14]

When, in 2017, PCS entered the merger with Agrium, not for US$38.6 billion, but for the equivalent of US$14 billion in Nutrien shares, the idea that the head office of Nutrien would be more than nominally located in Saskatoon was not on the radar screen. Saskatchewan is not the centre of their universe, although they will say nice things about the province when they fly in. They just can't see themselves living there.

The question of head office, as previously discussed, is of interest to the Saskatchewan people. It also may affect how the people and the government of the province think of and relate to the industry. There's a real difference between a publicly owned corporation, or even one seen to be headquartered in Saskatchewan or with Saskatchewan roots in its DNA on the one hand, and a corporation that is really a foreign entity on the other.

Although the industry is greatly consolidated, the branch plants are gone, and there are only a few players left, Saskatchewan is back to the 1960s in the sense that potash producers' senior corporate managers do not have a strong connection to the province. Given that the two major ones are large multinationals with diversified interests, they probably never will. Of course, the mines are here. The mining jobs are here. Some head office–type functions are here. But the decision-making is not here. The idea that Nutrien is a Saskatchewan company first and foremost has no traction. In fact, Nutrien, although engaged in the mining of potash, is not first and foremost a mining company. Potash mining by Nutrien is part of a huge vertically integrated diversified conglomerate. Saskatchewan's largest potash asset, the former PCS, is now part of the company whose main business is not potash mining.

Perhaps the loss of participating in or influencing decisions concerning how the potash industry would operate in Saskatchewan, and in relation to the world market, was inevitable after privatizing PCS. In her 1986 study, published at a time Devine's Progressive Conservative government was in office but had not yet sold PCS, Olewiler considered whether privatization would be in the province's interests. She noted the companies paid their taxes and complied with regulations and were able to successfully operate after PCS was created. She noted that PCS gave the government a "window on the industry" in the sense that government would be aware of the costs of extracting potash. She concluded: "Privatization of PCS would definitely hinder moves to achieve 'orderly behavior' in the provincial industry. Without the government as a major holder of potash assets, it is difficult to see how the province could persuade private producers to act in the best interests of Saskatchewan residents."[15]

After PCS was privatized, the Saskatchewan people still felt that PCS was somehow their company, even though that was not the case. With the merger of PCS into Nutrien, there is no entity to which the province has a connection. The potash industry is entitled to expect to be treated fairly and reasonably but should also expect the provincial government to make hardheaded decisions where the public interest needs to be advanced. The government should always push the public interest envelope, not simply give big business what it wants. The people of the province have the right to expect that there is a respectful, but not cozy, relationship between their government and big business.

Regardless of political beliefs, people in Saskatchewan would agree that the public is entitled to a reasonable share of profits from resource extraction. What is reasonable should be determined according to a reasonable return for the potash mining companies, entities that are no longer seen as part of the family any longer. It should be okay to insist that excessive profits should belong to the public, not to the companies. Chapter 8 will present the financial picture to provide you with accurate information so you can form your own opinion as to what is reasonable.

One doesn't have to be a social democrat to believe that the government should ensure maximum public benefit from potash mining, whether publicly or privately owned.

FIVE

POTASH MINES CAN'T BE MOVED TO CHICAGO

SERVING IN GOVERNMENT IN THE LATE 1990S AND EARLY 2000S, I learned potash mines in operation for decades needed to be retooled. As well, investment was needed to expand productive capacity in the province.

I knew that if the oil and gas sector wasn't happy with the government, they could apply pressure by shutting down their wells, adversely impacting both employment and spinoff economic activity from suppliers and retailers of all sorts. It was very difficult, however, for potash companies to make multi-billion-dollar investments in potash mines and shut them down because they don't like government policy. The capital investment required is simply too large to allow them to play those games for very long, because the cost of doing so is too high.

After Bill Doyle became president and CEO of PCS in 1999, an introductory meeting with Premier Roy Romanow was arranged. While sometimes bringing together two strong and somewhat charismatic personalities is the start of a cordial relationship founded upon mutual respect, the meeting did not have that outcome. Disagreement over head office jobs going to Chicago and other matters led to a very animated and frank exchange of views, in which Doyle, true to his American citizenship, provided a skeptical analysis of the premier's political philosophy. The premier conveyed his certainty that although PCS Inc. might move every corporate executive to its Chicago office, the corporation would be unable to move the mines there, and those would have to remain within the jurisdiction of the government of Saskatchewan.

It was good that these gentlemen were able to have this dialogue, since the opportunity to do so never arose again in the remaining few years that Romanow served as premier. During that time, the company was able to continue hollowing out decision-making authority at its nominal Saskatoon head office but, as the premier had predicted, it was unable to take the mines outside the province.

Premier Brad Wall momentarily seemed prepared to assert himself where potash was concerned. In a 2015 *Globe and Mail* article, Sean Silcoff noted: "Potash Corp. is one of the squeakiest wheels in Saskatchewan politics. For once, it's nice to see the government push back a little. Mr. Wall can afford to: it's not like Potash can shut its mines and move them to another country."[1] Ironically, the pushback Silcoff refers to was the commitment in the 2015 Saskatchewan budget to conduct a review of potash royalties and taxes. Minister of Finance Ken Krawetz stated there would be "a broader review of the entire potash tax and royalty regime [to] balance the excellent investment and operational environment for this sector, which is so important to the provincial economy, with the need for a fair return for the owners of the resource, the people of Saskatchewan."[2]

Like Silcoff, Jack Mintz publicly commended Premier Wall for finally calling for a review. Once the idea of a review of potash royalties and taxes was mentioned, it seemed to disappear, and before long, as will be discussed herein, Premier Wall was able to say the province received a good return without the necessity of a review.

I had my own differences of opinion with Doyle, although we managed to remain on good speaking terms. I tried to point out to the PCS board that Saskatoon should be where its senior executives were located. In 2006, I wrote a letter to Dallas Howe, chair of the PCS board, and copied it to each member of the board, including Doyle. I suggested the hollowing out of the corporate suite in Saskatoon was a violation of the legislation requiring the PCS head office be in Saskatchewan—or at least it violated the spirit of that provision.

As I was Saskatchewan's finance minister and then industry and resources minister over a combined span of ten years in those two portfolios, meeting or talking on the phone with the CEOs of major companies in Saskatchewan (and sometimes elsewhere) was not unusual. There were always issues of concern to them, perhaps impacting the corporate bottom line or perhaps impacting the level of employment they could offer workers in Saskatchewan.

One day, after my letter to the PCS directors was sent, I got a call from Doyle, who is usually a very well-spoken and convincing person. Although our points of view diverged on a number of issues, we got along quite well, and our exchanges were usually pleasant.

My letter to the PCS board had obviously irritated Doyle. He said the letter had made the directors nervous about the company's relationship with the government and that it had not been necessary for me to worry the directors. He said I should have picked up the phone and called him if I had a concern. I'm not sure what that would've accomplished, since Doyle was responsible for what I was complaining about and, even in our conversation, wasn't offering to change the situation, notwithstanding the fact that he had already received and read my letter about it. I said I thought I made a valid point and it needed to be shared with the directors, who are collectively responsible for the company. I said I would take his suggestions under advisement.

Doyle became quite animated during the call. It became clear that he was also upset because of a recent Saskatchewan trade mission to India I had led. The mission included an entrepreneur trying to establish a new potash mine in Saskatchewan and seeking investors or potash customers in India.

"You're trying to steal our customers away," Doyle said to me. I explained that although I had attended a meeting where the businessperson made a pitch for investment or customers, I made it clear at the meeting that this was a private initiative, not an initiative of the Saskatchewan government, and that the government neither endorsed nor opposed it. I had followed up with a letter to the people concerned in India when I got back, just to make sure there was no misunderstanding. I told Doyle that people were free to attempt to develop mines or go into business. I said the Saskatchewan government appreciated the important contributions the potash producers made to the economy of Saskatchewan and employment in the province, but that it was not a closed shop, and if someone wanted to try to establish a potash mine, they were entitled to do so. On reflection, I could have added that I hoped PCS was as appreciative of all the contributions of Saskatchewan people to PCS as I was of PCS's role in the provincial economy.

Doyle was not quite mollified by my comments. He said words to the effect of "let me tell you something. There is no one that can build a potash mine in Saskatchewan except PCS." He explained that no greenfield operation was possible because it couldn't compete with existing, already-paid-for mining infrastructure, which can be a platform for expanding existing (or "brownfield") operations. The cost to develop a greenfield mine was too expensive, and such a mine would not be able to compete with the existing producers. He added that, if a greenfield mine was ever built in Saskatchewan, it certainly would not be built by the businessperson in question. Given his adamant assertions that no competing mine could be built and that the proponent of the mine could not build it, I'm not sure what all the fuss was about.

Doyle continued to assertively express his consternation at what he perceived to be my lack of appreciation for the potash producers and became fairly agitated. Having made his points about the letter to the board of directors, and the presence of a want-to-be potash miner on the trade mission, he next decided he would let me know his views about my politics. He said, "I know all about your party. Your party passed legislation in the 1970s authorizing the government to expropriate the potash industry." This was stated in a manner that suggested he had discovered a secret I was not aware of, and he was now letting me in on it. Up until that point, I had been mainly just listening to Doyle blow off steam. I said, "Bill, now let me tell you something. If you are referring to some steps Allan Blakeney took in the 1970s to establish the Potash Corporation of Saskatchewan, supposedly headquartered in Saskatoon, I am familiar with that history. And, if Allan Blakeney had not negotiated the purchase of five potash mines to create PCS, there would be no Potash Corporation of Saskatchewan, and you, Bill, would not be the president and CEO."

At that point, Doyle, who had been speaking fairly loudly, paused, and after a few seconds replied very calmly and nicely, "Well, Eric, I guess you're right about that." I never asked Doyle if the corporation ever celebrated Blakeney's contributions, and Devine's in a different manner, at the head office in Saskatoon, or in Chicago.

In the early 2000s, government believed the forty-year-old mines should be retooled, and we wanted Saskatchewan's position as the world leader in potash production maintained by incenting multi-billion-dollar investments in refurbishment and expansion. If we achieved that, the industry would be here, it would be here for decades more, and it would not be in a position to shut things down. We wanted to provide an incentive package that would accomplish the goal of expansion, and, while we wanted the royalty and taxation structure to bring about a fair return to the people of the province, the main priority at that time was not higher revenues to government, but expansion. The investment could not be driven by profit alone at that time because the companies were not making huge profits. Negotiations between the government and industry, which took place for several years in the early part of the twenty-first-century, were not about taxes and royalties for the most part. We were not in a situation of what could be considered windfall or extraordinarily high profits to the industry. The focus was upon building up the industry again, just as it had been a priority of the Thatcher and Blakeney governments in the 1960s and 1970s.

No one in either industry or government anticipated that what subsequently happened to potash prices would occur. One of the things government officials achieved in negotiations with PCS, Agrium, and International Minerals and Chemical Corporation (IMC, now part of Mosaic) was a capital cost allowance of $1.20 for every dollar of capital investment. Jack Mintz of the University of Calgary's School of Public Policy described this as overly generous.[3] Perhaps it was overly generous, and I don't claim everything I was responsible for in government was perfect. One thing I can claim is that it seemed to work.

The companies committed to the government that, if we brought in a new set of incentives and reduced royalties on new production, they would invest at least $2 billion over five years. As prices ballooned, so did plans for expansion. Given the original commitment of $2 billion in infrastructure investment, rising prices clearly had a huge impact on investment decisions. In the first few decades of the twenty-first century, producers invested approximately $20 billion in expansions and, in the case of K+S, in a greenfield mine. In 2005, Agrium and PCS had a combined productive capacity of 12.3 million tonnes, rising to 13 million tonnes by 2020 and projected to be 18 million tonnes by 2025. Mosaic's capacity would be 8.4 million tonnes in 2005, 10.5 million tonnes in 2020, and a projected 12 million tonnes in 2025. K+S produces about 2 million tonnes, which may rise to 3 million tonnes by 2025. BHP expects the initial capacity of its Jansen mine to be 4.35 million tonnes. The combined result is that capacity of about 20.7 million tonnes in 2005 rose to 25.5 million tonnes by 2020 and could be 37.35 million tonnes in 2025, representing an almost 84 percent increase in productive capacity from 2005 to 2025.[4]

A Government of Saskatchewan news release described the $12 billion BHP Jansen potash mine as "the single largest economic investment in Saskatchewan history."[5]

Existing producers had a great advantage because they had infrastructure in the form of shafts and underground shops, etc., which were paid for years before, and which involved investments of hundreds of millions of dollars and a replacement cost would be in the billions. This made it difficult for new entrants to build new mines and compete effectively. At a meeting with executives of the companies and public servants one day, I asked why they had formulated a draft incentive for expansions (or brownfield development) but had no provision for greenfield development. "What if someone wants to build a new mine?" I asked. The answer from both government and industry was an immediate "That's not possible, Minister." I accepted that. It had a logical basis, since if you looked at the price of potash at the time, it was hard to see how the cost of a new mine could be paid and a profit generated. Neither the industry nor government officials anticipated the price increases that took the average yearly price from $216 per tonne in 2004 to an average of close to $600 per tonne from 2008 to 2022 inclusive.[6] Industry was able to operate at a profit when the price was at the $200 to $300 dollar per tonne range.

The question may be asked why it would be necessary for the Government of Saskatchewan to provide incentives for investment in potash mine refurbishment and expansion when, after all, Saskatchewan has the best quality potash in the world, the largest reserves, and has political stability and rule of law. When the choice is really between investing in Russia and Belarus versus Saskatchewan, let's face it, there really is no choice. So why in the world would we need to incentivize investment?

The world was somewhat different in the early 2000s. Prices were not high, and profits were not huge. The money needed to refurbish and expand the potash sector was in the billions. We had not experienced multi-billion-dollar investments in potash before the twenty-first century. The sort of capital required is global capital. Capital will flow to where it makes the largest return. That's a natural and understandable fact. It is, after all, a capitalist system. If an investor wants to invest in potash, clearly Saskatchewan is the best place to do it. However, money doesn't necessarily go to a particular sector like potash. If a higher profit can be made in something else, capital will go there. It certainly was not the case in the early 2000s that potash would be where capital would make the biggest return. That situation changed dramatically, and no one predicted it. Therefore, we wanted to be sure that we would incentivize large investment in potash.

Another logical question to ask would be: If you believe that public ownership of part of the potash industry was a good thing for the province, why didn't you do that?

I have no doubt that public investment and ownership in potash was a wise decision, and that the province would be much better off if PCS had not been privatized. That has always been my belief.

If we had wanted to get into potash, we wouldn't be able to, as we didn't have the financial capacity to do so. Certainly, in the early 1990s, it would have been totally out of the question since the province was practically bankrupt. At one point, we had to ask Brian Mulroney's Conservative government in Ottawa to give us $50 million or we would have defaulted on bond payments that were coming due. Defaulting would have had bad consequences for not only Saskatchewan but also the country, and the federal government was no more interested in seeing that happen than the provincial government was.

In any discussion about the government acquiring assets of any sort from private owners, the discussion should always assume that the fair market value for the asset will be paid. We live in a society governed by the rule of law, and people have the right to expect that the product of their work and investment will not be subject to arbitrary confiscation without fair compensation. Perhaps the only exception would be with respect to windfall profits, since the governments of Alberta and Saskatchewan did, in fact, confiscate the companies' contractual right to have royalties capped at a certain level. In this situation, however, clearly the profit had not been acquired solely through the investor's efforts. While the capture of windfall profit is fair game, government should pay fair market value for assets privately owned. If and when government determines it is in the public interest to take privately owned mining assets into public hands, fairness and maintenance of a reasonable investment climate demand such payment. As well, if tax incentives have been provided to encourage capital investment, companies should expect a return on investment commensurate with reasonable expectations at the time the incentive and investment initiatives were arrived at. Unusual and unexpected developments may lead to windfall profits, and governments may act due to changed circumstances. Government should not reverse commitments given in the absence of unexpected developments. As will be explored further in this book, an economic rent approach would provide stability by linking taxation to price and profit fluctuations, with revenue to government automatically adjusting to an appropriate level commensurate with market conditions.

Probably the financial impediment to public investment could have been overcome if there had been the political will to do so, and the province could have acquired part of the potash industry and done very well in terms of returns to the public treasury. It was still not feasible, simply because there was and has not been a demonstrated consensus of Saskatchewan people to provide government with a mandate to be directly involved in ownership of the resource sector. In politics, you have the opportunity to speak to a large number of people almost on a daily basis. Judging by the fact that virtually no one called upon government to get involved in the resource sector directly, and many comments were made to the contrary, there appeared to be little appetite for government to get into the potash business or the oil business. The Saskatchewan public views utilities that serve them directly as appropriate areas for Crown ownership—but not necessarily other forms of enterprise. The political environment of the 1990s was not the same as in the 1970s, when Canadian nationalism and concern about foreign ownership were regularly matters of discussion, and public ownership seemed to be more actively debated and under consideration.

Remember that the Blakeney government of the 1970s involved the province also in the oil business through the Crown corporation SaskOil. It was a successful business that helped develop Saskatchewan's oil sector and gave the government a window into the industry. The government may not have had as high a profit margin as major private producers, but it did make a profit, all of which was retained in Saskatchewan.

My personal philosophy is like that of Blakeney's, in that I believe returns to the Saskatchewan people are maximized when the public owns a share of our unusual endowment of potash and oil. I believe that our society has many unmet needs, which could be met with additional resources we would gain through direct involvement in the resource sector. I do not agree with the view of many conservative people that such a policy scares off private investors. Capital will always come in if it can make a good return. All we have to do is look at many countries in the world where government is involved in the resource sector and where private investment is not deterred. We do not need to bow down to Toronto's Bay Street or to Wall Street.

It is an interesting situation to be in government and to occupy positions like minister of finance or of industry and resources and to pursue policies that, on one level, are not the ultimate ideal in your personal opinion, but, on another level, you see as the best approach to take. You have to respect that you govern for the province as a whole. There was no apparent public appetite for public ownership in the resource sector. Regardless of my personal beliefs, I tried to proceed in a manner that was respectful of people from all political persuasions. To some extent, you can lead by moving society to a position that challenges some basic assumptions and beliefs and makes change possible. Blakeney's government certainly dramatically tried to do so. You cannot, however, lead people to a place they do not want to go. It was clear that the Devine government's privatization of PCS in 1989 had not led to much outcry at all, and there was no indication that the public wanted the NDP government to redo what had been undone.

A person in government may have views that are not in accord with most of the population. In one sense, when you don't act on those views, your actions are not consistent with your personal beliefs. However, if you wish to serve the public, engage in public life, and pursue the public interest as best you can, you seek to do what is realistic and attainable to improve life in your jurisdiction. It was my view, shared by colleagues in the Legislative Assembly and Cabinet, that the people of Saskatchewan wanted good jobs for their children and grandchildren. If you wanted to make society better, you wanted a healthier economy producing wealth, which would hopefully result in a better situation for people generally.

In arriving at public policy that serves the public interest, realistic options are assessed and what seems to be the best one chosen. The goal of social democrats to redistribute wealth is best served if you have policies in place to create wealth and a healthy economy. A healthy private sector and a robust public one is a good combination. We needed to further develop the potash sector and conventional oil production. There are many people on the left side of the political spectrum who are pretty good at talking about how wealth should be redistributed, and how money should be spent on education and health care, but not so good at describing exactly how and where we're going to get the money. The policy arrived at to encourage expansion of the potash sector contributed positively to economic growth and helped create an even bigger potash mining sector in Saskatchewan. The benefits of that growth are not being adequately shared with the Saskatchewan people, and that is the issue the province faces today.

It is not a contradiction to want healthy private industry and a healthy public treasury. You need both. Balance is always desirable. Sometimes, given my middle-of-the-road approach, NDP colleagues would get frustrated with me. On one occasion, a colleague in the legislature got mad at me in a caucus meeting when I was presenting and debating with him a tax change that I proposed. He said: "All you ever do is talk about business and taxes!" This was stated as if I were doing something quite wrong and were insensitive to the needs of the people.

I replied: "Well, we have a caucus of thirty people. Twenty-seven of you talk about spending money on health, education, social services, and the like. Three of us—Eldon Lautermilch, Maynard Sonntag, and I—talk about business and the economy. I think that's a fair balance."

Centre-left governments need a few social democrats with a fairly strong interest in the private sector, reward for hard work and innovation, and wealth creation. Conservative governments, conversely, need to have a few members who are socially progressive and have a good sense of how public policy can lift people up. They need people who realize the market economy is not going to achieve adequate results all by itself. Both the left and the right run into trouble when they neglect a balanced approach in either direction and seek to have only like-minded "yes" people adhering to some particular partisan perspective or ideology. Like everything in life, balance is important.

It appears Scott Moe's government is too ideologically driven, in the sense that it does not seem to fully understand the need for an appropriate balance between corporate profit and public good. The government appears to believe that anything that is good for big business is good for the province. But again, balance is needed. Just as the NDP needs to look for policies that encourage economic growth, the Saskatchewan Party needs to focus on the extent to which extreme corporate profit is acceptable when there are people living in abject poverty, education is underfunded, and the health care system is in crisis. Government should not be overly pro-business or pro-labour but focused on the broad public interest. As will be asserted in the remaining chapters, the needed balance between the private sector and the public sector is absent.

Returning to where this chapter started, I felt that the best thing to do was to have the potash industry seriously rebuilt and expanded in the province. We made an arrangement with the potash companies. They said that if we agreed to do these things, they would invest $2 billion over the next five years. When I was introducing the changes, one of my colleagues said to me, "They'll never do it." I said I thought they would, and, in fact, the $2 billion became $10 billion over five years, and the $10 billion doubled to $20 billion, contributing to growth in the Saskatchewan economy from about 2007 on. Investment in potash mine expansion in 2007–2022 was in the range of $30 billion, with up to $12 billion to be spent on BHP's Jansen project in the coming years.[7]

In the years 2007–2020, capital construction spending in Saskatchewan rose dramatically, from about $8.6 billion to $11.3 billion from 1998 to 2006, to a range of $10.6 billion to $23.9 billion from 2007 to 2020, the last year statistics are available at the time of writing. The average expenditure on capital construction for 1998 to 2006 was $9.5 billion. For the period after 2007, when potash expansion projects were mainly underway, average capital construction spending was $18.1 billion. Capital construction spending rose steadily from 2007, peaking in 2014 and then generally falling until 2020.

As construction capital spending rose, the GDP of the province did as well. As it ebbed from its peak in 2014, the provincial GDP growth became GDP reductions for all but two years in the 2015–2020 period.

Potash construction capital expenditure does not comprise all or even most of the increased spending of that type for 2007–2020 and represents about 20 to 25 percent of increased spending. The point here is simply that such spending has a positive impact on GDP numbers. To look at it another way, for the initial period of 1998–2007, construction capital spending represented 16 percent of provincial GDP. For the years 2008–2020, it accounted for 25 percent of the provincial GDP. Growth of the province's GDP in this period was in large measure due to capital construction projects, and potash mine expansions (along with new mines built by K+S and still under construction by BHP) were an important factor in that growth.[8]

Maybe the capital cost allowance was too high. Maybe we didn't design the system in the best possible way. One thing I know for sure is that an industry exists in Saskatchewan that is not going anywhere and will continue to produce and employ people in the province for generations to come. I have an issue with the way in which the profits are being distributed. That can be fixed. We should expect government to want to fix it, and we should expect an industry that approaches the issue in a manner respectful to the people of the province.

In retrospect, knowing what has occurred in the world potash market since 2005, I believe the tax concessions to the potash companies to spur expansion were too generous. The expansions would have eventually occurred in any event to meet world demand. The planning and construction would have started somewhat later but eventually would have occurred. At the time the policies were implemented, however, there weren't high prices for potash or windfall profits. If that situation had continued, investment without the incentives would not have occurred, and decisions were made in that context. However, on reflection, the incentives were necessary at that point but likely could have been less generous.

Hindsight is always twenty-twenty and you make the best decisions you can based on the evidence before you and the advice you receive. The future is unknown and uncertain and can be full of surprises.

You can stand still forever if you only do what is 100-percent consistent with your personal philosophy and a 100-percent certainty. You should never violate your core values and beliefs. At the same time, however, you are of no use if you cannot do what is best under the circumstances. You assess the situation, decide what the possible options are, try to choose the best one, and proceed. Usually, you will not get everything quite right, and there will be room for criticism. Mistakes will be made, and lessons will be learned. Still, you cannot stand still and fail to collaborate with people in government and elsewhere to do what you can. On balance, Saskatchewan has achieved a great thing. We have the world's best potash industry, which, unlike its largest competitors, is in a free and democratic society governed by rule of law.

SIX

INTEGRATION OF THE POTASH CORPORATION OF SASKATCHEWAN INTO NUTRIEN

A S LONG AS THE PRICE OF POTASH WAS SUCH THAT BILL DOYLE DID not have to worry about any new potash mines being feasible, Saskatchewan potash producers could carry on without looking over their shoulders. Excess capacity to produce potash in Saskatchewan could usually be put to use in the market to prevent the price from getting so high that potential competitors could start looking at getting into potash mining. The price of a metric tonne of potash rose from US$112.50 in 2002–03 to US$152.50 in 2005, gradually increasing to US$240.00 in March 2008. Over the next year, it spiked at US$682.50. It stayed there until the middle of 2009 and dropped to US$312.50 over the next year. Even with that drop in price, a tonne of potash was worth twice as much as it had been five years before.[1]

Just as lower prices would make new mines unfeasible, higher prices would have potential competitors looking at developing new mines or would make existing producers attractive targets for a takeover or merger. Now there was considerable interest by a bunch of start-ups hoping to get into potash, and some major players too. K+S, a German potash and salt company that had been a partner in Alwinsal, the original developer and operator of the Lanigan potash mine, started to consider a new mine in

55

Saskatchewan. BHP, one of the world's largest mining companies, had no potash assets, but saw the mineral as an opportunity and wanted to get a piece of the action. To do so, it could either buy a producer or develop its own mine. Since developing a mine is costly and presents uncertainties, the option of buying a potash-producing company could be a more attractive option. And in a free market economy with free market governments in Ottawa and Regina, BHP approached PCS and conveyed an interest in doing so.

Rebuffed by the PCS Board, which felt that BHP's US$38.6 billion offer was an attempt to "steal" the company, BHP presented PCS shareholders with an offer to buy their shares at US$130 per share.

To prevent this "steal" from occurring, leaving PCS intact to merge eight years later with Agrium in return for approximately US$14 billion in shares of Nutrien, less than half of the amount offered by BHP, Saskatchewan Premier Brad Wall helped lead the charge to convince Conservative Prime Minister Stephen Harper's federal government to not allow BHP to acquire shares from PCS shareholders. The premier said potash was a strategic resource for Saskatchewan. This is true because it is valuable, and Saskatchewan has enough to supply the world for a thousand years. The public owns the vast majority of the potash reserves in the ground. The difference if large pools of capital outside Saskatchewan owned the mines through foreign-owned PCS or foreign-owned BHP was never made clear. Nor was it made clear eight years later why Saskatchewan was better off having half of its strategic resource subsumed into a vertically integrated fertilizer company rather than a company more focused on potash mining. That was not even the subject of comment by the Government of Saskatchewan. Premier Wall did not like BHP's plan to market potash itself rather than through Canpotex, which sold (and continues to sell) potash on behalf of the two major Saskatchewan producers in offshore markets. The argument was that Canpotex had its office and employed people in Saskatchewan. BHP committed to having its potash division headquartered in Saskatchewan and employing marketing people there. It would be relatively easy to locate BHP's potash division in Saskatchewan since it didn't have one anywhere else. In fact, it could have a larger presence in Saskatchewan than PCS still had or Nutrien might have. The arrangement the government might have been comfortable with could have been negotiated with BHP. The power of the province to set taxation and royalty rates put it in a position to obtain the arrangement it wanted.

While BHP's hostile bid was still in play, I was retained by a US advisory firm to meet by telephone various investment bankers from New York several times. They wanted to discuss what the chances were that government would block the deal. They made very large investment decisions on behalf of their clients, such as large pension funds, based in part upon their assessment of likely market developments. These were people who controlled billions of dollars in investment capital. At the beginning of the process, I said that PCS was upset about the bid and had a connection to Saskatchewan, but we had market-friendly governments in both Regina and Ottawa, so I felt it was 60 percent likely the government would let the shareholders decide if they wanted to sell to BHP.

As I listened to provincial politicians and the Saskatchewan media over the following weeks, my view shifted to 55 percent in favour of the federal government blocking the deal, and that's what I advised the investment bankers. They seemed very dubious about what I was saying, and I got the impression they thought I really didn't have a good handle on the situation. Maybe they had heard of my association with a political party that gave itself legislative power to expropriate potash mines in the 1970s.

The bankers said the scenario I described would be a very strange result from a Conservative government. Free marketers believe in the marketplace making market decisions, not government, they said.

Except when they don't.

It turned out that I was right, although I didn't take any particular pleasure in that.

Meanwhile, the people of the province were strongly behind Premier Wall's stance. They seemed to feel that Saskatchewan was losing our potash to some big multinational, not acknowledging that potash itself always belonged to the people of the province, and a Saskatchewan entity owning the mines had effectively ended almost 30 years before.

People spoke as though Saskatchewan was losing mines it didn't own and losing a resource, which it would in fact continue to own. BHP had offered the shareholders $130 per share at a time when the shares were trading at about $117. The share price quickly rose to about $156 before the government blocked the bid. Doyle, usually a reliable and staunch advocate of the free market, and not a big fan of government intervention, seemed happy to have the provincial government assist in convincing Ottawa to stop the "steal." Doyle called BHP's offer grossly inadequate and a substantial undervaluation of the company.[2]

Years later, BHP's offer could be seen in a different light. PCS shares dropped to less than half their 2010 price after the rejection of BHP's bid. "Retail shareholders today can only weep at the memory of BHP's US$130-a-share offer price."[3]

In fairness to Doyle, it was not he who eight years later would lead PCS into a merger that valued shareholders' assets at less than half the amount BHP offered. If the matter had been left for the shareholders to decide, perhaps BHP would have had to pay US$160 or more per share. By the time PCS was absorbed by Nutrien, each PCS share was valued at 0.4 of a Nutrien share. The shares had by then been split into three, so this was the equivalent of 1.2 shares of Nutrien. The original price of Nutrien's shares was about US$55, so basically PCS shareholders got US$66 per share rather than US$130 to US$160.

Perhaps BHP's initial offer wasn't really as hostile as everyone seemed to think in 2010. Its attempt at theft, as well, seems in retrospect to have been somewhat ham-handed.

No one complained about PCS management's advice to shareholders and governments or questioned shareholders not being allowed to deal with their shares. PCS directors and the provincial and federal governments were all free marketers after all. If they didn't know what they were doing, who did?

No one seemed too concerned about high market prices attracting new entrants into the business or what the implications of disallowing the BHP bid might be. No one seemed to question if decisions made in corporate board rooms or by government served to maximize shareholder value or were best suited to serve provincial interests. Later, no one would seriously question the PCS decision to merge with Nutrien, or if that was good for Saskatchewan's strategic resource.

By the end of the twentieth century, the original ten potash mines built by nine separate companies were in the hands of PCS, which owned five; Mosaic, which owned four; and Agrium, which owned one to support its distribution of fertilizer. PCS was the largest potash mining company in the world. This ownership situation and PCS's status remained the case at the time BHP made its hostile takeover bid in 2010.

Premier Wall did extract from PCS a Pledge to Saskatchewan to address some concerns about the actual presence of PCS in the province, given the removal of most executive decision-makers to Chicago. The Pledge to Saskatchewan committed PCS to the following:

- PCS or any buyer of PCS would maintain the company's headquarters in Saskatchewan.
- The CEO, CFO, and president of PCS Potash would all "maintain residency in Saskatchewan."
- More than 200 employees would work at the Saskatoon corporate headquarters.
- Canpotex would continue to handle offshore sales.
- An Aboriginal Engagement Strategy would continue to be developed.
- Charitable contributions would continue, with PCS as the "number one corporate citizen in Saskatchewan in terms of philanthropic giving."
- Local purchasing would be pursued as possible.
- The ongoing and planned capital expansion projects would be completed.[4]

In a letter to Premier Wall dated February 14, 2011, Doyle provided more details of the pledge. Now there would be at least 300 employees in the Saskatoon office by the end of 2013, up from 209 at the end of 2010. There would be 11 of 14 senior executives working in Saskatoon by the end of March 2012, up from 6. The workforce at the mines would be increasing from 2,016 workers to 2,528 workers by the end of 2015. As well, one percent of before-tax revenue would go to charity and community organization, and the STARS air ambulance organization would be one of the charitable commitments of PCS.

Doyle stated: "We understand the strong and mutually beneficial role that our company plays in the province, and we will always seek to do what is right for the people of Saskatchewan and the company's stakeholders. On behalf of everyone at the Potash Corporation of Saskatchewan, we look forward to continuing to play a vital role in the Province of Saskatchewan for decades to come."[5]

Well, sort of. Effective January 1, 2018, PCS and Agrium, in what was described as a merger, came together. PCS and Agrium shareholders were given Nutrien shares to replace their shares in the former companies. This development represented a major change not only to Saskatchewan's potash industry, but also in the world market for potash. Up until then, PCS operated with a focus on potash mining. It had other divisions, including nitrogen, phosphates, animal nutrition, and industrial chemicals, but potash mining was at its core and the foundation of its profitability and success. Agrium, with its one potash mine and phosphate and nitrogen divisions, was (and Nutrien now is) the world's largest fertilizer distributor. It had always operated the Vanscoy mine as part of Cominco as a source of potash, but it was not primarily a potash miner, or really even a mining company per se.

The PCS and Nutrien merger did not give rise to many questions on Saskatchewan's interests that required answers or cause the province to elicit any iron-clad guarantees. Premier Wall stated he expected the new Nutrien to honour "the spirit and the letter" of PCS's Pledge to Saskatchewan.[6]

The pledge of course was that PCS or a buyer of PCS would have its head office in Saskatchewan, and this would include the CEO, CFO, as well as the president of the Potash Mining Division and the majority of senior executives.

Premier Wall said Minister of Energy and Resources Nancy Heppner was going to contact PCS and Agrium "to ensure the new firm's head office will in fact be located in Saskatchewan."[7] He said he wanted "to ensure that Saskatchewan, as the head office for this company, has the maximum number of head office jobs, that the presence in this province is indisputably the head office."[8]

Once again, it appeared Premier Wall was standing up for Saskatchewan in the face of this merger. Then things started to get a bit murky. Randy Burton, speaking on PCS's behalf in an emailed statement, "did not say where Nutrien's senior executives will be based, but emphasized that the merger will not affect the company's 'approach to Saskatchewan or any other jurisdictions' where it operates."[9] Of course, the statement Nutrien would act in the same manner as PCS could be taken in more than one way. And since the new entity had to carry on in the same way in various jurisdictions, it would be doing so in not only Saskatchewan but also Alberta, where Agrium's headquarters were located. Although Nutrien's head office was "indisputably" in Saskatoon, since it calls that office the head office, the Pledge to Saskatchewan for "decades to come" included

specific references to the aforementioned positions and that those holding these positions would be residing in Saskatchewan, along with Doyle.
Eleven out of fourteen senior executives of the company would be in
Saskatoon. Nutrien has fallen somewhat short of fulfilling this commitment. Notwithstanding the loss of PCS as a company focused on potash
mining, and its conversion to a division of a giant fertilizer conglomerate,
no assurances were obtained, even after the company explicitly declined
to give a commitment that the Pledge to Saskatchewan would be honoured either in spirit or by the letter of the pledge, or indisputably.

A month after Premier Wall said he expected the pledge to be honoured, he again addressed the matter. In September 2017, he said he would
not rule out using legislation or the potash royalty structure "to maximize
the number of corporate headquarters jobs in Saskatchewan."[10]

Even as Premier Wall once again appeared to be taking the corporate giants on, he already knew the pledge would not be honoured. By
then, Nutrien had announced that its CEO, Chuck Magro, would maintain his residence in Calgary. Premier Wall said this was "not optimal."[11]
Meanwhile, Alberta's NDP economic development minister was quoted as
saying it would be "business as usual" for employees located in Alberta.[12]

Perhaps that resulted from an Agrium Pledge to Alberta? Agrium's vice
president of investor relations "declined to put numbers on the current
complement of employees in PotashCorp's Saskatoon headquarters or at
the Agrium head office in Calgary."[13] Perhaps everyone had been too busy
preparing for the big merger to do a head count.

Premier Wall, meanwhile, had already expressed displeasure in 2013,
when PCS laid off 18 percent of its workforce to cut costs to meet what
Doyle described as a "sacrosanct" imperative for shareholders to receive
a planned dividend.[14] The Pledge to Saskatchewan stated PCS would not
only maintain, but also expand jobs.

After Premier Wall fought off BHP along with PCS in 2010, after he
received the Pledge to Saskatchewan and the details that followed, after
he saw what the pledge meant in terms of both jobs and the presence
of senior executives in the upcoming "indisputable" head office, it would
have been understandable for him to make good on his statement that all
options would be pursued. Instead, he backed off on the royalty and tax
review promised in the 2015 Saskatchewan budget and, a few years later,
brushed aside the growing list of experts pointing out some problems with

the tax and royalty system. He opted to echo the potash industry's views that there was no need to alter Saskatchewan's tax and royalty system (as will be discussed in chapter 8). There were no entreaties to Ottawa to stop the merger, and no pursuit of options to enforce the spirit and the letter of commitments given to Saskatchewan in return for its efforts to thwart the BHP bid of 2010.

Nutrien noted in its 2019 annual report:

> Nutrien is the world's largest producer of potash with approximately 21 percent of global potash capacity. We have access to decades of low-cost reserves from our six potash mines in Saskatchewan....Nutrien's Potash mines represent some of the lowest-cost and highest-quality mines in the world.[15]

Whether or not it was in Saskatchewan's interests to have its highest quality mines provide lowest cost potash to its new owners was never the subject of any known expression of concern by the government of Saskatchewan.

Nutrien's managers will do what managers of publicly traded companies should do. They will maximize profits. What is best for Saskatchewan is not their responsibility. While the province has an interest in keeping mines going and people employed, and local communities have an interest in having good jobs in the community, Nutrien's job is to maximize profit. It isn't their job to decide what is best for Saskatchewan or what the province's share of the profits should be. That's the job of the Saskatchewan government and its electors. In expressing the view that events have not transpired in a way that is most advantageous for the people of Saskatchewan, I do not place responsibility for that on the shoulders of Nutrien. They are doing what they should do.

Nutrien's annual reports set out its objectives. They include an economical source of fertilizer for farmers, mainly in the United States, and cost savings through automation. From Nutrien's point of view, lower labour costs and higher profits are good for the shareholders. Questions such as how much will be saved, how much more wage income for Saskatchewan workers will be paid if greater automation is not pursued, how much income tax is lost to government, and what the impact is on communities close to the potash mines are not primary considerations for private potash producers. Once it was decided it wasn't the government's role to be an owner in the potash industry, are the chips just left to fall where they may?

Nutrien's market cap, or total value of shares, is over $30 billion, while Mosaic's is in the $12 billion range.

Nutrien is now the largest potash producer in the world, as well as a producer of phosphate and nitrogen. It is also the world's largest fertilizer retailer. That makes Nutrien vertically integrated: it extracts raw products to make fertilizer and other products it sells. It is the miner, the processor, the wholesaler, and the retailer all in one. It owns retail outlets throughout North America that sell fertilizer and other products to agricultural producers.

As such, Nutrien's outlook is not simply that of a potash producer wanting to keep profits from potash high and considering only what is good for potash mining. It has other priorities, one of which is to have an economical supply of potash to support its wholesale and retail operations. Nutrien's priority is not only a good price for potash, but also a good source of potash for its other activities. Its focus cannot be solely on what is good for potash mining in Saskatchewan, although that will of course be one factor. Nutrien has other irons in the fire, since it is not just a producer of potash, but actually a consumer as well. In a 2020 *Globe and Mail* article, Joel Jackson of BMO Capital Markets said that the merger of Agrium and PCS in 2018 was more of a takeover of PCS.[16]

"This was not a merger. This was Agrium taking over PotashCorp," Jackson is quoted as saying. He noted that Agrium executives ended up taking most of the key positions, and operations would effectively be run from Calgary.

As of 2018, a potash corporation "of Saskatchewan" no longer existed. It was subsumed into a new entity. In addition, the PCS mines are no longer operated by a mining company; they are now in the hands of a fertilizer conglomerate. These changes are significant. That aspect did not draw any attention from the government of Saskatchewan or the Saskatchewan media. As noted in the *Globe and Mail*, "Agrium brought a mentality to the business that was different from that of a straight materials producer like PotashCorp. For them, the commodity itself is not so valuable as the relationship with the end customer—the farmer. 'This is a commodity business, but relationships in the ag business matter,' [then Nutrien CEO Chuck] Magro told a conference in Florida last February, highlighting the fact that, through its retail division, Nutrien has a direct connection to half a million farmers in seven countries."[17]

It took a Toronto publication to point out what had actually happened to the largest potash producer in the world. It no longer exists as a potash producer per se. It is gone. Fifty years before, the government of Saskatchewan determined that decisions in the potash industry and market required a Saskatchewan presence to pursue the goal of maximizing benefit for the people of the province through revenue, jobs, and economic development. With the creation of Nutrien, decisions impacting the health of the industry and economic development in Saskatchewan would now be made by the world's largest fertilizer company and would represent what was best for it and its farmer customers in the United States. Concerning both the fate of the world's potash producer and the maximization of a return to the people of the province, the government of Saskatchewan demonstrated no apparent concern, at least none that was ever followed up on. The prevailing view seems to be what is good for multinational conglomerates must be good for the people and province of Saskatchewan. It is as though to be open for business, what business is doing should not be questioned. Unless, apparently, business itself asks government to intervene in the market.

In 2010, BHP's offer to pay PCS shareholders US$38.4 billion was described by Doyle as an attempt to "steal" the company. The governments of Saskatchewan and Canada, as well as the corporate executives at PCS, were having none of that. In 2018, Nutrien's absorption of PCS into a fertilizer retailer resulted in PCS shareholders being given shares in Nutrien valued at around US$14 billion, less than half of what BHP had offered to shareholders in their opening bid. Neither this fact nor the fact that the mining sector would become an appendage of a fertilizer giant seemed to raise any issues with PCS executives or the Saskatchewan government. How this represented maximization of shareholder value or a deal that recognized potash as a "strategic resource" for Saskatchewan has never been explained or even discussed publicly. With respect to both the BHP attempted takeover of PCS and the PCS merger with Agrium to form Nutrien, the government of Saskatchewan seemed to completely agree with what PCS executives had to say about each deal, regardless of the impact on shareholder value or Saskatchewan having a role to play in the world potash market, and in spite of breaches of commitments made to the people of the province in return for the government's efforts in 2010.

Both BHP and Nutrien would be owned by external shareholders, essentially mainly by the same large pools of capital. In the case of Nutrien, however, the conflict between mining and consuming potash existed. BHP, on the other hand, is a mining company and would focus on the health of the mining sector. And it would pay more than double what Nutrien paid in the 2018 share swap. Yet "BHP is bad, Nutrien is good" seemed to be the approach, with no discussion of any of the implications.

When PCS became part of Nutrien, it was assigned a market cap or value of US$14.3 billion, compared to the lesser amount of US$13.7 billion assigned to the other party to the merger, Agrium. Despite that, it is PCS which really lost its identity when the merger occurred. It was the largest potash miner in the world, with five Saskatchewan mines. It also made and marketed fertilizer and associated products. Agrium wasn't simply a commodity producer. "It's a mining company, yes, but also a manufacturer, a retailer, a financial institution and even a software-as-a-service provider. And this ever more vertically-integrated model—instituted through what some describe as a management coup—has brought stability its predecessor PotashCorp never knew and size alone could not deliver."[18]

Agrium was much more diversified than PCS with the above components as well as its nitrogen and phosphate plants and an extensive network of farm supply outlets in North America and other continents.

As reported in the *Globe and Mail*, former Nutrien CEO Chuck Magro saw it this way: "The investment that has actually taken place since the merger...has been almost entirely in retail."[19] The article noted that "Nutrien has also built a sideline in customer finance. Currently lending to 20 percent of its customers," though Magro wanted to grow that to 50 percent.[20] The article went on to note that "the largest single capital allocation in 2019—32 percent of free cash flow—went toward share buybacks."[21]

As Magro put it, "The integrated model we've built—that is where the true value comes out."[22]

One could be forgiven for thinking Saskatchewan's priorities are not on Nutrien's radar screen, judging by its initial corporate reports. The new owner of half of Saskatchewan's potash industry noted in its initial *2018 Annual Report* that world population is rising, the demand for protein is growing, and the amount of arable land available is shrinking. Nutrien reported it has positioned itself as "the largest global agricultural retail network, creating a strong relationship with and channel to the grower."[23]

The grower is not, for the most part, the Saskatchewan farmer, but the US agricultural producer. Nutrien's stated focus, as the world's largest potash producer, is not potash production. Its focus is on the ultimate sale of agricultural products to growers. Nutrien describes its vision to be "the leading global integrated ag solutions provider."[24] Producing potash is an important component of providing solutions, but it is a part of a bigger picture. As its 2022 *Annual Report* notes, Nutrien acquired "existing low-cost potash capacity."[25]

Neither the stated focus nor the vision of Nutrien as described includes Saskatchewan's principal interests. One could even be forgiven for thinking Nutrien was not sensitive to Saskatchewan's priorities. The Nutrien 2018 *Sustainability Report* states: "In 2018, we took significant time and effort to assess our sustainability priorities as a new company." This time and effort included engagement with internal and external stakeholders to identify sustainability topics highly relevant to Nutrien and the stakeholders. External participants included the following:

- customers
- suppliers
- NGOS
- investors
- Indigenous groups
- communities
- industry
- government (a former member of Canadian parliament/former minister of state for finance).[26]

That this is a description of what a resource corporation operating in the province of Saskatchewan regards as an example of consultation with key stakeholders, including government, is mind-boggling. Nowhere is the government of Saskatchewan mentioned as having been consulted, or as a party that might have views on topics of "high relevance" relating to sustainability and potash mining. These could include topics such as employment in the province, environmental stewardship, community investment, stable production, and avoidance of layoffs, not to mention taxes, royalties, and other revenue to the province. Somehow, the single biggest stakeholder where Nutrien is engaged in potash mining—the government of Saskatchewan—does not warrant a mention. Instead, bizarrely, even though natural resources are within the constitutional control of the province, not the government of Canada, it was apparently thought that a federal politician would represent government as a stakeholder. This strange notion is made even stranger when it is indicated that the person whose views were sought is a "former" member of parliament, not even a current member of the federal government. It is presumably a person not associated with the current federal government, but a previous government. Saskatchewan in 2018 didn't have any former federal government ministers other than members of the Conservative government, which had not been in office since 2015. This inexplicable description of consultation with "government" is strange enough already without considering that the former politician reportedly spoken to had no apparent responsibility for natural resources or the environment at the federal level, not that that would have made much difference since the federal government plays practically no role when it comes to regulation of potash mines.

Nutrien absorbed PCS. PCS certainly had some knowledge of the importance of the government of Saskatchewan to the world of potash mining. Nutrien missed, or at least failed to mention, the obvious need to respect the province that provides it with mineral leases and the permission to operate, and determines royalties and taxes. On that basis, it would seem Nutrien's stated "significant time and effort" to assess "sustainability priorities" may not have been time and effort well spent. Five minutes spent with anyone somewhat familiar with potash mining in Saskatchewan would have been more instructive. It doesn't matter if it is stated that Saskatchewan contains the "head office" of Nutrien if the decision-makers don't really have a focus on Saskatchewan.

The government of Saskatchewan may wish to bring several matters to Nutrien's attention, as topics of "high relevance," perhaps including consideration of a review of royalties and taxes as a key priority.

After the 1989 privatization of PCS, there was a Saskatchewan connection with the primary decision-makers. With Nutrien, if its first indications accurately reflect its mindset, the province doesn't even get that. Nutrien has captured potash as part of a much bigger play, and Saskatchewan needs to recognize that and make hard-headed rational decisions that are best for Saskatchewan people. Nutrien needs to be informed of the province's interest in jobs, revenue, procurement from Saskatchewan businesses, community investment, research activities, and value add. It needs to be informed of the fact the province has an interest in decisions which will affect the world market and avoid or ameliorate the boom-and-bust cycle to the extent possible to promote job stability and avoid layoffs. It could also be mentioned that Nutrien's plans to increase automation to increase profits would not be viewed favourably if increased shareholder value comes at the expense of decreased employment and a smaller paycheque in the province.

As CEO of PCS, Bill Doyle routinely lobbied government to allow a small potash research staff in Saskatoon, funded largely by the Saskatchewan government through tax credits to the potash companies, to be moved to Atlanta, Georgia. He proposed they would still be paid by the province through the tax credits. As the minister responsible for approving the annual budget for the research operation in Saskatchewan, I refused these requests. Doyle thought I "didn't understand the big picture." Maybe so, but it seems to be getting clearer all the time.

In addition to having a source of low-cost potash, Nutrien has a stated goal of lowering the cost of production through data analytics and automation.[27] Nutrien's *2022 Annual Report* states: "Our most significant achievement in 2022 was to remove more employees from the active mining face by achieving over eight thousand employee hours of tele-remote and autonomous mining."[28] It is not hard to understand the corporate objectives of increasing safety and lowering cost, and if the measure is necessary to improve the safety of workers then that is commendable. If it ultimately results in job losses, it is fair to assume, however, that Nutrien's analysis of the net benefit of automation will not be as sensitive to the need for high salary jobs in mining as the government of Saskatchewan should be, and as communities close to the mines are. Nutrien needs to bear in mind that the province may at some point decide it wishes to assert itself. Ownership of the mines is gone. The head office has been effectively removed. Higher profits have been relinquished to the shareholders. Nevertheless, at some point Saskatchewan might draw the line at job losses. It might decide that Nutrien's bottom line should not be the only consideration. The Saskatchewan treasury may come up with a bottom line, or working families, or communities, or citizens generally.

At the end of the day, the province still owns the potash. That's a very important bottom line.

CONSEQUENCES OF CHOICES MADE IN 1989, 2010, AND 2018

T IS PART OF THE GOVERNMENT'S RESPONSIBILITY TO CREATE AN environment where industry can sustainably and profitably operate and, in the case of resource corporations, to maximize return from the sale of the province's resources. Those running publicly traded companies will advance the interests of the companies they work for to maximize shareholder value. That's their job. They will push the envelope forward and try to get lower taxes and better incentives from government. It is government's job to push the envelope back where necessary in the public interest.

Governments in Saskatchewan have a curious track record when it comes to maximizing benefit from Saskatchewan's world-class potash resource and ensuring the province has some say when decisions affecting it are being made.

Grant Devine's government sold off PCS, a profitable Crown corporation, for $630 million in 1989. A few years later, in 1997, PCS had a market cap ten times higher. Even those who argue the Saskatchewan public should play no role in owning part of the potash industry should agree it was unwise to sell PCS at the bottom of a severe downturn in the potash market. Why not hang on until some additional value could be obtained for the largest potash company in the world?

If selling PCS in 1989 was a good business decision due to the prospects for potash being in doubt because the whole industry was in the doldrums in the 1980s, it would be reasonable that other owners of potash mines in Saskatchewan would also recognize that and dispose of their assets after years of no or low profits as well.

But none of them did. The private companies running the Colonsay, Vanscoy, Belle Plaine, and the two Esterhazy mines did not sell. Kalium Chemicals Ltd., which owned the Belle Plaine mine, did sell to IMC in 1995, but by then the landscape had changed considerably, and they got money for value. Only the Saskatchewan government saw it as a good idea to sell its potash mines in 1989. It is not unreasonable to conclude that this was a decision driven more by ideology than business considerations or basic common sense.

As previously noted, the offer to buy PCS in 2010 was US$38.6 billion. That was another strange year of decision. Nothing like that amount offered was ever captured for PCS shareholders, who were deprived of the opportunity to say for themselves if they wanted to sell their shares to BHP. In retrospect, BHP's US$38.6 billion offer doesn't look so bad, given subsequent developments associated with the emergence of Nutrien in 2018. PCS's share price at the time of the BHP offer was $117. BHP's initial offer was $130 per share, but that was their initial offer. The PCS share price rose to $156 per share after BHP's offer and perhaps BHP would have put more on the table. After BHP was disallowed from dealing with the shareholders, PCS's share price dropped to less than half of the $156 value. It cannot be ruled out that the prospect of BHP having to get into potash by building its own mine or mines placed downward pressure on the PCS share price. Similarly, the Mosaic share price of $76.36 at the end of 2010 dropped steadily to $11.91 in May 2020 before recovering to $40 in early 2023.

Perhaps those losses of shareholder value are not all that relevant to the people of Saskatchewan, given that the shareholders of PCS and Mosaic don't reside within the province to any appreciable extent. Other factors, however, also make the rejection of BHP questionable. BHP is one of the world's largest mining companies. It was public knowledge it planned to get into potash mining. Nutrien, by contrast, is the world's largest fertilizer company and now owns the largest potash mining entity in the world. Saskatchewan's primary interest is in the health of the potash mining industry—more than the fertilizer wholesaling and retailing industry. In that sense, BHP would have been a better fit for Saskatchewan.

The result of the BHP bid being disallowed was that if BHP was to pursue its stated objective of getting into potash mining, it was left with no option other than to build its own mine. PCS is now gone, and Mosaic, although publicly traded, is controlled by a small number of shareholders with large holdings and not easily susceptible to a hostile takeover bid. Any takeover of Mosaic would have to be a friendly one. Questions about whether a giant new mine will cause oversupply in the world market, and whether that would be beneficial to other potash producers, workers in the industry, or the Saskatchewan economy did not appear to be given consideration. Perhaps it was not foreseen that BHP might decide to build its own mine, or it was seen as a possibility, but the huge capital investment required was seen by government as a welcome development, notwithstanding possible oversupply. Certainly, BHP's Jansen project has turned out to be a long-term development. The first stage of the development began in 2012. With the project on the long-term horizon since then, current and future investors in PCS and Mosaic, and now Nutrien, must be wondering what impact new production from Jansen would have on the potash market.

As of January 1, 2018, the absorption of PCS into Nutrien went ahead as planned. The province, notwithstanding Premier Wall's statements, as well as the federal government, took a fairly hands-off approach and did not ask any of the hard questions. And questions do seem to arise.

As previously discussed, Nutrien noted in its 2019 annual report that it had access to "decades of lower-cost reserves from our six potash mines in Saskatchewan,"[1] and that its mines were low cost and of the highest quality. The integration of PCS into the new entity was key to the emergence of a fertilizer giant, with the major goal of "integration and innovation across our supply chain and our approach to market."[2]

Whether or not it was in Saskatchewan's interests to have its highest-quality mines provide access to Nutrien of low-cost reserves and obtain lowest-cost potash for its fertilizer was never the subject of any known expression of concern by the Saskatchewan government.

It was undoubtedly a good fit for Nutrien, just as PCS in 1989 was a good investment opportunity for the private investors who ended up owning it. These "highest-quality mines in the world" owned by Nutrien were put together as a powerful unit by the people of Saskatchewan. Their sale for

US$38.6 billion to a mining company was blocked. They were merged into a vertically integrated corporation whose stated goal is to own the production facilities for the components of fertilizer, not to optimize profit from mining. This was done in 2018 and cost Nutrien US$14 billion. If BHP had acquired PCS, it would be selling the potash to multinational fertilizer companies. Instead, Nutrien operates the mines and does it as part of its integrated approach. Nutrien can use the potash in its own operations and decide what is best in wholesaling and retailing fertilizer in terms of having the most cost-effective approach for farmers mainly outside of Canada. This was definitely a strong advantage for Nutrien. Whether or not it is a strong advantage for Saskatchewan is highly debatable.

The model of resource management for Saskatchewan potash, if there is such a model, does not seem to result in maximum returns for the people of the province. Though advocates of full private ownership claim that the trickle-down theory applies and somehow dividends paid to shareholders in New York, Toronto, and elsewhere trickle down to the people of the province, unfortunately, that is not reality.

In saying the rejection of BHP as a potential owner of the six PCS mines seemed to have occurred without consideration of all the implications for potash mining, supply, and price; the value of PCS shares; and the impact of potential new mines created by BHP, I do not mean to say BHP's presence in Saskatchewan is a bad thing. My point is that I am not sure the rejection of the BHP bid by PCS and the government of Saskatchewan considered all the implications. There would be no harm to the interests of the people of Saskatchewan if BHP owned the potash mines, since the public's status as owners of the potash itself would not change. Regarding the role of Canpotex and how potash produced at BHP mines was marketed, the government had the option of making an arrangement with BHP. What the pros and cons of BHP developing potash mines in Saskatchewan are will not be completely known until it actually occurs and maybe for years after that. BHP's ongoing construction at its Jansen site, where ultimately an estimated $12 billion will be spent on the first stage, has and will continue to have a positive impact on Saskatchewan's economy. It will provide hundreds, if not thousands, of jobs in the development stage, and eventually, hundreds of jobs in potash mining on an ongoing basis.

BHP has an opportunity to be seen to recognize Saskatchewan as a great place to live by having an effective head office of its potash division in Saskatchewan. True, Mosaic employs dozens of people at a corporate office in Regina in addition to hundreds at its mines. Nutrien now employs about 400 people in office jobs at its nominal head office in Saskatoon. The senior executives and decision-makers of those companies are, however, almost entirely located outside Saskatchewan.

It may seem counterintuitive to state that a huge company like BHP, which dwarfs Mosaic and even Nutrien, might have a more meaningful head office presence in Saskatchewan. Without a doubt, BHP will continue to have large offices in places like Melbourne, Australia; London England; and various other places. However, if BHP is as serious about building a potash business as it evidently is, it should build a new potash division. It could choose to make its Saskatoon office a robust head office for what would essentially be its world potash division, located within the province. It is highly likely that all of BHP's potash production will be in Saskatchewan. Its marketing network would extend into the United States, as well as offshore. If it chooses to continue doing its own marketing rather than through Canpotex, there is no reason the marketing arm could not be headquartered in Saskatoon. If BHP placed the senior decision-makers of its potash division in Saskatchewan and truly gave Saskatchewan a recognized world headquarters for its potash division, it could replace the now-gone PCS in the hearts and minds of the Saskatchewan people as a corporation seen to be closely connected to the province, a place good enough to extract resources from and good enough to live in.

Another positive consequence of the rejection of BHP and its entry as a potash miner in Saskatchewan was that the sheer enormity of the productive capacity being built in the province cements the reputation of the province as the place to "do potash" in the free world. It achieved the original objectives of the policies of Ross Thatcher's Liberal government, Allan Blakeney's NDP government, and Lorne Calvert's NDP government in the early part of the twentieth century to expand productive capacity in Saskatchewan. It represented multi-billion-dollar developments that cannot be moved anywhere else and therefore meant thousands of highly paid jobs in the province on an ongoing basis in Saskatchewan's potash mining industry for a long time to come.

It should also mean a good return to the provincial treasury. Another approach that would endear BHP to the people of the province would be a realistic assessment of what profit share should be between the company and the provincial treasury, rather than efforts to defend a tax and royalty system that is untenable and indefensible.

Whether or not the expanded productive capacity of Saskatchewan's potash mines will be good or bad in the short or long term is anyone's guess. No one, including the CEOs of large mining companies paid millions of dollars per year, can predict the future. The oversupply of the late 1960s was overcome as Saskatchewan established its reputation as a potash supplier. Increased production may result in what PCS as a Crown corporation planned to do, which was to earn money from volume rather than price. Increased production at a lower price may allow potash companies to profit but perhaps not at the levels we presently see. Perhaps the price will drop from current levels. This is not necessarily a bad development in terms of the ability of the industry to operate profitably and could be a good development in terms of less affluent countries being able to produce food for their citizens. We cannot forget that while we in North America generally live with an abundance of food and water, if we ignore the needs of people around the world, we may be faced with international conflict over world resources.

The opposition by PCS executives and the Saskatchewan government to the attempt of BHP to bargain with PCS shareholders had consequences. To say that is not to say the consequences will be necessarily bad or necessarily good. Arguably, the consequences for PCS shareholders were not good. It is perhaps more important that the position of PCS resulted in a major new player entering the Saskatchewan potash mining industry, with its own productive capacity and with significant impact on Saskatchewan's economy and the potash market.

THE PROFITS OF POTASH

THE BLAKENEY GOVERNMENT OF THE 1970S OBTAINED A FAIR return for the potash Saskatchewan mining companies extracted, which was one of its stated objectives. The government policy at that time was that revenues going beyond the cost of potash mining plus a reasonable profit should substantially benefit the people of Saskatchewan as owners of the resource.

The percentage of potash sales per year producers paid to Saskatchewan's public treasury in royalties and other forms of taxation was 1.91 percent in 1971, the year Blakeney became premier. By 1974, it was 11.1 percent, and an average of 21.25 percent was achieved between 1975, when the government created PCS, and 1982, when Grant Devine's Progressive Conservatives swept to power.[1]

During the Conservative government's tenure of 1982–1991, the public's share of the revenue from potash sales ranged from 6.1 percent in 1983 to a high of 8.94 percent in 1988 and averaged 6.77 percent.[2] To be fair to the Devine government, the 1980s were not good years for the potash industry. The value of production fell from over $1 billion in 1980 to a low of $542 million in 1986, not topping $1 billion again until 1994.[3] It can reasonably be expected that hard times will impact both the potash companies and the public treasury.

It might also be reasonably expected that a return to good times would benefit both foreign shareholders and Saskatchewan citizens. In real dollar terms, taking inflation into account, the value of potash sales did not really reach the 1980 level until 2005: $1 billion in 1980 was the equivalent of $2.37 billion in 2005.[4] That year, the value of potash sales reached $2.7 billion. After 2007, both potash prices and the value of sales skyrocketed, reaching $3 billion that year and $7.5 billion in 2021, and almost $18 billion in 2022.[5] The price of potash doubled and tripled after 2008, which created a whole new set of circumstances, urgently calling for reform of the province's potash royalty and tax system to more fairly compensate the people of Saskatchewan. The current system was not set up to deal with the level of profit the industry is making and, as will be discussed below, this has been the case for about fifteen years.

Appendix A to this book, which is summarized in table 1 below, shows the value of sales from 1963 to 2022, and royalties, taxes, and surcharges paid to the public treasury, both in dollars and as a percentage of sales.

Five-year averages of sales value, revenue to the companies, and percent of value received by the public treasury are as follows:

Table 1. Value of Potash Sales, Payments to Public Treasury, and Public Share as a Percent of Value of Potash Sales (Yearly Averages over Five-Year Periods)[6]

Years	Value of Sales (Can$ million)	Public Revenue (Can$ million)	Percent Revenue to Sales (%)
1963–1967	48.00	1.04	2
1968–1972	107.00	3.20	3
1973–1977	320.60	65.90	21
1978–1982	770.59	170.20	22
1983–1987	653.00	44.36	7
1988–1992	828.00	57.12	7
1993–1997	1,150.00	128.36	11
1998–2002	1,680.00	187.05	11.1
2003–2007	2,350.00	339.76	14
2008–2012	5,700.00	622.28	11
2013–2017	5,270.00	517.27	10
2018–2022	8,600.00	1284.47	15

The public's share of the value of potash sales as determined by the government did not increase during the last few decades, even though circumstances had changed significantly, with the prices and profits doubling, tripling, and then some. This chapter details company profits; the concept of economic rent for resource extraction will be discussed later. At this point, I am simply noting that where profit is made not as the result of risk, investment, or innovation but simply from a higher market price, such profits should belong to the owner of the resource and not simply be kept by the mining industry. The average share of potash sales paid to government for the years 2008 to 2017 was about 11 percent, below the averages achieved in much less profitable years, such as 1998 to 2007. In the profitable years of the 1970s, government obtained a share of value that was twice as high for the people of the province in percentage terms than what is being collected today.

Global population and the demand for food have grown steadily, as has the world's understanding of and use of nutrients such as fertilizer. Thanks to the investments of the potash companies, which are acknowledged and need to be factored into any calculation of a reasonable rate of return, Saskatchewan has potash mining infrastructure that is second to none in the world. The province has a robust, efficient, world-class, and market-influencing potash mining sector.

The productive capacity objectives of past Saskatchewan governments have been achieved. What has not been achieved is past governments' goal to maximize public benefit from Saskatchewan's potash resource. Political leaders have been largely silent on this issue for some time or, when pressed, have indicated that no change in public policy or taxation of potash companies is required. The job of ensuring revenue to the public is commensurate with the value of potash given up has been avoided for the last decade and a half. The province's ability to ensure decisions influencing the market for potash are sensitive to Saskatchewan's interests is not assured and, judging by the lack of follow-through on the Pledge to Saskatchewan, could be seen as ineffective. The caveat, however, is that if a Saskatchewan government wants to assert itself in the interests of the people of the province, it has the powerful tool of being able to assess royalties and taxes. It is never too late to change course.

For at least a dozen years, various experts have been alerting the government and the public that the province is being seriously short-changed. Voices such as Duanjie Chen and Jack Mintz of the University of Calgary's School of Public Policy[7] and Jim Marshall of the University of Regina/University of Saskatchewan Johnson Shoyama Graduate School of

Public Policy[8] have factually documented the pressing need for a review of Saskatchewan's royalty and taxation policies.

As early as 2010, Jack Mintz was writing that Saskatchewan's potash tax and royalty structure was not working and "fails to collect rents properly." His solution: "A proper potash royalty to collect rents could apply to business cash flows."[9]

In 2013, Chen and Mintz authored a paper that states Saskatchewan's royalty and tax system for potash "has actually reached the point of incoherence and absurdity, or a mess."[10] As will be documented in this chapter, at the time the 2013 study was produced, profits were already in the windfall category but had not yet soared to the even higher levels they have since. Therefore, if the authors found the system to be an absurd mess in 2013, it has become something even more lopsided since. In a 2015 paper, the same authors speculated that the province's abundance of a natural resource as valuable as potash may have "engendered an approach whereby tax policy has not been considered a top priority."[11]

This chapter presents charts showing potash sales figures for PCS and Agrium from 1995 until they merged into Nutrien in 2018, and its potash sales since then. The chapter also presents the potash sales of Mosaic, the other large potash producer, as well as its predecessor IMC. Although K+S Potash Canada has been producing potash from its Bethune mine since 2017, figures on its sales and profits from Saskatchewan production are not presently available due to aggregated statements prepared in Germany, where the company operates other potash mines. Information on the financial returns from the Bethune mine has not been accessed.

It should be noted that all figures, except as indicated, are from corporate annual reports and filings, or Saskatchewan government annual budget documents.

Also important to note, for the purpose of context, is that these figures do not represent the total amount of the revenue or gross profits of PCS, Agrium, Nutrien, IMC, or Mosaic. They reflect only the portion of corporate revenue and gross profit derived from potash sales, which are almost totally from Saskatchewan.[12] The actual revenues and gross profits of each of those companies are higher than the figures presented here because they all also engage in enterprises beyond potash. No attempt has been made to claim the people of Saskatchewan should be rewarded for activities of the companies not directly related to Saskatchewan potash.

Although an argument can be made in PCS's case that public ownership could have resulted in the same complementary activities that PCS has successfully developed, and the development of which was underway when it was still a Crown corporation owned by the Saskatchewan public, that argument is not part of this analysis. If it was, the loss to the people of the province demonstrated here would be even higher.

The foundation of PCS and the reason for its huge success as a privately owned company is rooted in the actions of the Saskatchewan government, which brought together the assets of several companies and created the largest potash producer in the world. A comparison of PCS's gross profit from its potash division to its gross profit overall shows that between 1995 and 2017, after which PCS became part of Nutrien, potash averaged 60 percent of the gross profit of PCS. The importance of potash was not eclipsed by diversification into other areas. In fact, in the years 2010 to 2017, potash accounted for 64 percent of PCS's overall gross margin.[13] The average percentages of gross profit from potash to overall profit were 59 percent (1995–2001), 56 percent (2002–2009), and 64 percent (2010–2017), the final year PCS was in business of its own accord.

Erin Weir is on solid ground in suggesting that the loss to Saskatchewan people from PCS's privatization would include profits from all of its divisions, not just potash.[14] That, however, is a different argument from this book's thesis. Public ownership of part of the industry may be an option. It is not necessary, however, to have public ownership to obtain some good value from Saskatchewan's potash resource. To fairly look at what additional amounts the province should be collecting from the potash companies, it is logical and reasonable to look at the profits the companies made from Saskatchewan potash. It is that commodity, and that value, that are strictly relevant to the discussion of what the province should receive through royalties and taxes. It is true that if PCS was owned by the people of the province, they would receive PCS's profits. What this book does is simply look at the profits earned from potash within PCS and the other potash companies and examine how those profits are shared between the companies and the Saskatchewan public treasury.

The big picture is that, from 1995 to 2017, PCS alone took in $20.56 billion in gross profits from potash, while the public treasury of Saskatchewan took from PCS, Mosaic, IMC, and Agrium combined, a total of $8.38 billion. The government does not release the amount of the payments each company made, for competitive commercial, and privacy reasons. If we assume PCS paid about half of the revenue to government, it would have paid royalties and taxes in the amount of about $4.6 billion. If PCS had been publicly owned, an additional $15.6 billion revenue to the people of the province would have resulted, all things remaining equal. However, what this book focuses on is simply the division of gross profits from potash between the companies and the government.

The figures presented in this book relating to PCS and the other companies are cautious and conservative, limited as they are to profits derived from Saskatchewan potash. PCS's total revenue and profit is not included in the calculations of profit contained in this chapter, even though, as Weir argues, all of it could be said to have been built on Saskatchewan potash and through the work of Saskatchewan people and their government. Additionally, although most of the potash produced by PCS and IMC/Mosaic is Saskatchewan potash, figures for those companies are discounted by an overly generous percentage accounting for production from New Brunswick for some years in PCS's case and from some production in the United States in IMC/Mosaic's case.

Even with an approach that does not include all profits of the potash companies, there is a large imbalance between the profits they make, as presented in the following pages, and the size of the return to the public as owners of the resource.

The potash sales figures of all companies, as reported below, are different from the yearly value of sales as reported by the government because the amount of potash the companies extract from the province in a year may be different from the companies' sales of the same year, since they may sell potash from a previous year, or they may be supplying it under longer-term agreements at a lower price than the then current market value. In such cases, the average price for that year would not be obtained. Gross profit amounts are a portion of the value of sales since the cost of production and the basic Crown royalty are deducted to determine gross profit.

The value of sales exceeded $7.5 billion in 2021 and reached almost $18 billion in 2022. It is noteworthy that, as PCS gross profits from potash rose, government revenue rose as well, but sometimes its percentage share of gross profits shrank.

No one would suggest that industry is not entitled to profit from its investment and for extracting, milling, and selling potash. The question is whether the people of the province are receiving a fair share of the profit, which results from high prices that reflect the inherent value of the potash being provided to the companies. Acknowledging the requirement that industry make a reasonable return on investment does not mean the level of profit should not be examined to determine if profit exceeds a reasonable rate of return.

Two legitimate interests need to be balanced: the potash company's interest in receiving a return on investment sufficient to justify a decision to invest in potash mining rather than other ventures, and the public interest in obtaining a fair price for providing the non-renewable resource, to ensure, to the extent possible, the public receives maximum benefit from its resources to meet the needs of Saskatchewan people and provide a legacy fund for the future. Readers can examine the situation for themselves and arrive at their own conclusion as to whether the appropriate balance has been achieved and whether the needs of Saskatchewan people are being met from the province's potash legacy.

In the following tables, the gross profit of potash producers is taken from the gross margin each company reported in its annual returns or US Securities and Exchange Commission (SEC) filings and includes sales revenue minus production costs and the basic Crown royalty.

Table 2 below contains annual figures for 1995–2017 for potash sales by PCS, discounted by 8 percent to account for possible sales from New Brunswick when in operation until 2015, and gross profit achieved from sales, expressed in both dollar terms and as a percentage of sales.[15]

Table 2. Potash Sales and Gross Profit for PCS Inc., 1995–2017

Year	Potash Sales (US$ millions) (.92 of actual for 1995–2015)	Gross Profit (US$ millions) (.92 of actual for 1995–2015)	Gross Profit as Percent of Sales (%)
1995	387.32	199.62	51.5
1996	370.94	175.34	47.3
1997	463.86	236.99	51.1
1998	501.85	291.02	58.0
1999	518.24	277.72	53.6
2000	532.40	279.67	52.5

Table 2. (*continued*)

Year	Potash Sales (US$ millions) (.92 of actual for 1995–2015)	Gross Profit (US$ millions) (.92 of actual for 1995–2015)	Gross Profit as Percent of Sales (%)
2001	483.46	222.44	46.0
2002	474.72	200.57	42.3
2003	521.46	187.41	35.9
2004	783.93	388.99	49.6
2005	1,070.79	647.93	60.5
2006	962.78	512.58	53.2
2007	1,441.18	835.00	57.9
2008	3,527.56	2,806.52	79.6
2009	1,109.24	680.29	61.3
2010	2,509.76	1,663.97	66.3
2011	3,427.00	2,500.68	73.0
2012	2,820.72	1,805.82	64.0
2013	2,476.64	1,457.25	58.8
2014	2,314.72	1,053.89	45.5
2015	2,127.04	1,228.15	57.7
2016	1,370.00	457.00	33.4
2017	1,628.00	804.00	49.4

PCS achieved average yearly gross profits of 48.78 percent of sales for the period 1985–2004, and 58.51 percent as prices and production rose after 2005 until the merger of PCS and Agrium into Nutrien effective January 1, 2018. In twenty-three years, from 1995 to 2017, the gross profit of PCS from potash was larger than the combined revenue from all potash companies to the Saskatchewan government in all but two years.

Except for the anomalous years of 2014–2017, Agrium achieved similar results, with an average gross profit of 46.37 percent for 1995–2004 and 56.57 percent for the period 2005–2013. Figures for 2014–2017 are related to expansion, construction activities, and shutdowns, and do not reflect normal activity.

Table 3 below contains annual Agrium sales figures for 1995–2017 for potash and gross potash profit, expressed in both dollar terms and as a percentage of sales.[16]

Table 3. Potash Sales and Gross Profit for Agrium Inc., 1995–2017

Year	Potash Sales (US$ millions)	Gross Profit (US$ millions)	Gross Profit as Percent of Sales (%)
1995	83.7	46.4	55.4
1996	78.3	32.2	41.1
1997	140.0	53.0	37.9
1998	160.0	69.0	43.1
1999	145.0	65.0	44.8
2000	151.0	70.0	46.4
2001	138.0	58.0	42.0
2002	158.0	67.0	42.4
2003	100.0	61.0	61.0
2004	214.0	106.0	49.5
2005	255.0	157.0	61.6
2006	213.0	98.0	46.0
2007	305.0	167.0	54.8
2008	816.0	632.0	77.5
2009	333.0	159.0	47.7
2010	675.0	371.0	55.0
2011	809.0	513.0	63.4
2012	618.0	342.0	55.3
2013	564.0	270.0	47.9
2014	391.0	70.0	17.9
2015	515.0	180.0	35.0
2016	419.0	52.0	12.4
2017	519.0	129.0	24.9

As can be seen in table 4, in its first years of operation, 2018–2022, Nutrien achieved an average of 61.78 percent gross profit from its potash sales.[17]

Table 4. **Potash Sales and Gross Profit for Nutrien, 2018–2022**

Year	Potash Sales (US$ millions)	Gross Profit (US$ millions)	Gross Profit as Percent of Sales (%)
2018	2,664.00	1,484.00	55.7
2019	2,603.00	1,501.00	57.7
2020	2,146.00	963.00	44.9
2021	4,036.00	2,751.00	68.2
2022	7,899.00	6,499.00	82.3

The gross profit as a percent of sales figures for 2021 and 2022 demonstrate huge windfall profits.

The figures for Mosaic, in table 5 below, are anomalous for the years 2014–2021 for reasons similar to the Agrium results for 2014–2017 due to intensive construction activity at Mosaic mines.[18]

Table 5. **Potash Sales and Gross Profit for Mosaic, 2005–2022**

Year	Potash Sales (US$ millions) (.90 of actual sales)	Gross Profit (US$ millions) (.90 of actual)	Gross Profit as Percent of Sales (%)
2005	773.46	221.52	28.6
2006	1,040.31	316.46	30.4
2007	1,331.01	372.51	28.0
2008	2,026.08	767.97	37.9
2009	2,535.48	1,355.31	53.5
2010	1,956.69	931.14	47.6
2011	2,754.93	1,322.82	48.0
2012	2,971.17	1,460.33	49.1
2013	3,176.37	1,450.01	45.6
2014	2,566.44	898.92	35.0
2015	2,202.30	709.47	32.2
2016	1,517.13	230.94	15.2
2017	1,667.31	352.44	21.1

2018	1,956.51	537.48	27.5
2019	1,902.42	555.21	29.2
2020	1,816.47	422.00	23.2
2021	2,364.12	951.75	40.3
2022	4,687.65	2,558.70	54.6

IMC was the predecessor operator for most of Mosaic's potash producing facilities. Because IMC and Mosaic accessed potash from United States mines, and it was not possible to obtain disaggregated financial information for product sales from Saskatchewan alone, 80 percent of IMC's sales volume is attributed to Saskatchewan mines, and 90 percent of Mosaic's, which would more than account for the value of any US production, considering volume and grade. Its Brazil production is accounted for separately. Gross profit figures for IMC were not obtained. For the purpose of this work, the gross profits of IMC were conservatively estimated to be 40 percent, below the average 48.78 percent gross profit achieved by PCS for the same period of production since 1995 and below Agrium's 46.37 percent during the same period. This would not be unfair to the potash producers and would not impact the overall analysis to any significant degree.[19]

Table 6. Potash Sales and Gross Profit for IMC, 1995–2004

Year	Potash Sales (US$ in millions) (.80 of actual sales)	Gross Profit at 40 Percent (US$ millions)	Gross Profit Assigned at 40 Percent of Sales (%)
1995	391.44	156.58	40.0
1996	371.84	148.74	40.0
1997	493.92	197.57	40.0
1998	560.08	224.03	40.0
1999	553.68	221.47	40.0
2000	696.80	278.72	40.0
2001	648.96	259.58	40.0
2002	644.72	257.89	40.0
2003	684.42	273.76	40.0
2004	696.00	278.40	40.0

The K+S Bethune mine has been in production since 2017. As noted elsewhere in this book, its potash sales and gross profits are aggregated in its financial statements with the figures from several other potash mines in Germany, so Saskatchewan numbers are not known. Production from the Bethune mine was in the range of 1.4, 1.9, and 1.6 million tonnes in 2018, 2019, and 2020 respectively, according to public disclosures in the annual reports of the K+S group of companies. Its 2020 production would amount to about 11 to 12 percent of the 13.7 thousand tonnes of Saskatchewan potash produced in that year.[20] The value of those sales, and payments to government, are included in the total value of potash sales and revenue to government presented in that table. The level of gross profit K+S achieved at this early stage is unknown.

A comparison of potash companies' gross profits from potash and payments to the Saskatchewan public for potash is as follows in table 7.

Table 7 demonstrates the combined gross profit of the companies for each year from 1995 to 2022 and the amount paid to the Saskatchewan government in each year for royalties and other forms of taxation.[21] Table 7 does not express the public share as a percentage of the gross profit each year because there is an overlap between gross profit and payments to government. Gross profit excludes basic Crown royalty payments but includes other forms of taxation not yet paid. For example, in 2015, gross profits were $2.7 billion. Payments to government were $736 million. If basic Crown royalties amounted to $100 million, then the companies would have had $2.8 billion in gross profit after deducting production costs but before deducting the basic Crown royalty. Basic Crown royalty payments, as a direct cost of acquiring and extracting the potash, are deducted from gross revenue. Other taxes are not. Without knowing which portion of the amounts paid to government is basic Crown royalties and which is other taxes, it is not possible to state precisely the percentage of gross profit paid to government, since the amount of the basic Crown royalty portion of gross profit is not known.

Therefore, this table accurately presents two sets of figures for illustrative purposes: gross profits exclusive of basic Crown royalty and taxes paid inclusive of basic Crown royalty. Notwithstanding that overlap, it validly portrays a pattern over periods of time, one of escalating gross profits with no exponential rise in payments to the public treasury. In the interest of precision, the overlap is noted; however, it does not detract from

Table 7. Industry Gross Profit—Industry Share and Public Share, 1995–2022[22]

Year	PCS (US$ in millions)	Agrium (US$ in millions)	Nutrien (US$ in millions)	IMC (US$ in millions)	Mosaic (US$ in millions)	Total (US$ in millions)	Total (Can$ in millions)	Public Share (Can$ in millions)
1995	199.62	46.4	—	156.58	—	402.60	552.49	136.90
1996	175.34	32.2	—	148.74	—	356.28	485.86	149.00
1997	236.99	53.0	—	197.57	—	487.56	674.93	160.40
1998	291.02	69.0	—	224.03	—	584.05	866.15	274.30
1999	277.22	65.0	—	221.47	—	563.69	830.84	228.45
2000	279.67	70.0	—	278.72	—	628.39	933.28	216.10
2001	222.94	58.0	—	259.58	—	540.52	836.06	238.65
2002	200.57	67.0	—	257.89	—	525.46	824.85	236.86
2003	187.41	61.0	—	273.76	—	522.17	741.64	188.93
2004	388.99	106.0	—	278.40	—	773.39	1,006.41	383.49
2005	647.93	157.0	—	—	221.52	1,026.45	1,244.06	374.94
2006	512.58	98.0	—	—	316.46	927.04	1,051.35	228.00
2007	835.00	167.0	—	—	372.51	1,374.51	1,475.68	524.47
2008	2,806.52	632.0	—	—	767.91	4,206.43	4,483.21	1,585.62

Table 7. (*continued*)

Year	PCS (US$ in millions)	Agrium (US$ in millions)	Nutrien (US$ in millions)	IMC (US$ in millions)	Mosaic (US$ in millions)	Total (US$ in millions)	Total (Can$ in millions)	Public Share (Can$ in millions)
2009	680.29	159.0	—	—	1,355.31	2,194.60	2,504.99	(-91.89)
2010	1,663.97	371.0	—	—	931.14	2,966.11	3,012.11	430.04
2011	2,500.68	513.0	—	—	1,322.82	4,336.50	4,289.66	643.97
2012	1,805.82	342.0	—	—	1,460.33	3,608.15	3,609.12	543.65
2013	1,457.25	270.0	—	—	1,450.01	3,177.26	3,273.21	514.33
2014	1,053.89	70.0	—	—	898.92	2,022.81	2,234.65	517.25
2015	1,228.15	180.0	—	—	709.47	2,117.62	2,708.71	736.07
2016	457.00	52.0	—	—	230.94	739.94	972.32	366.43
2017	804.00	129.0	—	—	352.44	1,285.44	1,668.63	452.28
2018	—	—	1,484.00	—	537.48	2,021.48	2,539.12	716.00
2019	—	—	1,501.00	—	555.21	2,056.21	2,779.93	733.03
2020	—	—	963.00	—	422.00	1,385.00	1,856.86	625.62
2021	—	—	2,751.00	—	951.75	3,702.75	4,642.14	1,453.50
2022	—	—	6,499.00	—	2,558.70	9,057.70	11,784.90	2,894.19

the analysis that revenue to the public treasury does not capture windfall profits. The imperfection in the amount of gross profit stated is constant throughout the years, and the relationship between the two sets of numbers is valid. As well, the result is consistent with the numbers contained in table 1 and appendix A, which set out the percentage of value of sales paid to government without any overlap.

It should be remembered that we have already very cautiously estimated potash producers' profits by generous exclusions to account for any potash that may have been obtained from New Brunswick or the United States where applicable, and by not taking into consideration profits PCS made from activities outside of potash extraction and sales, which arguably would have been payable to the provincial treasury had PCS not been privatized in 1989.

Even comparing provincial revenues (including the basic Crown royalty) to gross profits (that exclude it) indicates that, at least since the mid-1990s, the people of Saskatchewan have rarely received more than one-third of mine profits. If the Crown royalty was reported separately from other government revenues, adding it back into gross profits would reveal an even smaller public percentage.

Table 8. **Industry Profit Share and Saskatchewan Public Profit Share, 1995–2022**

Year	Industry Profit Share (Can$ in millions)		Saskatchewan Public Profit Share (Can$ in millions)	
	$	%	$	%
1995	552.49	75.2	136.90	24.8
1996	485.86	69.3	149.0	30.7
1997	674.93	76.2	160.40	23.8
1998	866.15	68.3	274.30	31.7
1999	830.84	72.5	228.45	27.5
2000	933.28	76.8	216.10	23.2
2001	836.06	71.5	238.65	28.5
2002	824.85	71.4	236.86	28.6
2003	741.64	74.5	188.93	25.5
2004	1,006.41	61.9	383.49	38.1
2005	1,244.06	69.9	374.94	30.1

Table 8. (*continued*)

Year	Industry Profit Share (Can$ in millions)		Saskatchewan Public Profit Share (Can$ in millions)	
	$	%	$	%
2006	1,051.35	78.3	228.00	21.7
2007	1,475.68	64.5	524.47	35.5
2008	4,483.21	66.6	1,585.62	33.4
2009	2,504.99	100.0	(-91.89)	0
2010	3,012.11	85.7	430.04	14.3
2011	4,289.66	85.0	643.97	15.0
2012	3,609.12	84.9	543.65	15.1
2013	3,273.21	84.3	514.33	15.7
2014	2,234.65	76.9	517.25	23.1
2015	2,708.71	72.8	736.07	27.2
2016	972.32	63.3	366.43	37.7
2017	1,668.63	72.9	452.28	27.1
2018	2,539.12	71.8	716.00	28.2
2019	2,779.93	73.6	733.03	26.4
2020	1,856.86	66.3	625.62	33.7
2021	4,642.14	68.7	1,453.5	31.3
2022	11,784.9	75.4	2,894.19	24.6

These tables illustrate that as gross profit has increased to very high levels, the percentage collected by the Saskatchewan Treasury Board Branch did not change appreciably or according to any coherent pattern. For example, in 1998, the industry made $866.15 million in gross profit by mining 8.04 million tonnes of potash. That amounted to about $108 per tonne. In real dollar terms, $108 dollars in 1998 would be worth about $177 in 2022.[23] If the potash companies made the same sort of profit they made in the past, in 2022, with increased production, they would have earned $177 times 14.4 million tonnes of potash produced for a total gross profit figure of $2.5 billion dollars. The gross profits of the industry in 2022 amounted to $11.8 billion. This profit per tonne of potash is 4.7 times higher than in 1998, even after adjusting for inflation. So taking account of increased production to 2022, it seems clear that there is a gigantic windfall profit involved in the business of potash mining in Saskatchewan.

The theory of economic rent is that the mining company should receive an adequate return on investment, and I doubt that anyone would be too upset if it was even a bit more than an adequate return. The rest should go to the owners of the resource. Revenue from increased price is a windfall to the industry. If not captured by the government (which it hasn't been), the industry has a windfall, and the people of the province are short-changed.

The reverse is also true: if there is a severe downturn and less money is made by the companies, then the public gets less in that instance. The point is that payments to both the industry and the public are tied to profit levels. Windfall profits, once increased costs of production are taken into account, should go to the owners.

In the 2023 Saskatchewan budget, the government celebrated that it had more resource revenue. Indeed it did. However, it should have been a lot higher. New revenue to the companies of close to $10 billion resulted in increased revenue to the public treasury of $1.6 billion, while the balance (84 percent) went to the potash companies.

It is surprising that no one in government seemed to take notice of record profits as a reason to take steps to increase the benefit to the Saskatchewan treasury, notwithstanding a government press release in March 2022, referring to decade-high price levels, strong market conditions, and an all-time high level of production.[24]

When a similar situation occurred in the early 1970s with very steep increases to oil prices and profits not due to any decisions, investments, or risk-taking by the oil companies, both the Progressive Conservative premier of Alberta, Peter Lougheed, and the NDP premier of Saskatchewan, Allan Blakeney, took the position that government should take the windfall profits for the public to receive payment commensurate with the value of the resource. The oil companies had drilled wells and made investments based on oil and gas leases that entitled them to pay royalties at a certain rate. The governments of Alberta and Saskatchewan confiscated those legal rights of the oil companies because dramatically changed circumstances dictated it was in the public interest that the wealth from public non-renewable resources should benefit the public first and foremost. Both premiers made changes to oil companies' rights to achieve that purpose—they did not hesitate. They did not worry whether they would be favourably viewed by oil companies and wealthy shareholders. They were more concerned about the public interest.

In the early 1970s, "Alberta was also moving (along with Saskatchewan) to recover a larger share of the returns generated from oil production. Standard Crown leases in Alberta allowed the province to take a variable royalty up to a ceiling of 16.6 percent of production." However, faced with oil prices rapidly rising after the "energy crisis," the Alberta government "enacted section 142.1 of the *Mines and Minerals Act* declaring all maximum royalty provisions to be void. It then implemented the new royalty scheme which boosted royalties substantially higher than 16.6 percent."[25] Saskatchewan took similar action.[26]

A precise assessment of exactly how much additional economic rent in the form of royalties and taxes the potash producers should pay to the people of Saskatchewan would involve an examination of the companies' detailed financial records and the application of specialized financial skills beyond the purview of this book. It is clear from readily available figures that profits exceed what is reasonable. Examination of financing and other costs that could be used to calculate a reasonable return on investment over time is required. The issue is sufficiently important that financial experts and government officials with access to all the information needed for a full analysis should be engaged to conduct a transparent and objective review in a manner seen to promote the public interest.

It is also clear, from numbers that are known and that provide the basis to apply a constant measure throughout the years, that revenue to and profits of the potash companies have risen dramatically in this century with no corresponding increase in the proportionate size of the public share, at a time when a large increase would be warranted. The annual value of potash sales and the amount of revenue paid to the government are contained in Saskatchewan government documents. They provide data on a consistent basis from which conclusions can be reliably drawn. They demonstrate that sales and profits have skyrocketed over the last twenty-five years. Meanwhile, the size of the public's share, as a percentage of the profits of the potash mining companies, has not grown appreciably.

Compiled from data in appendix A, table 9 shows average value of sales, average revenue to the public, and the percentage share of the public from 1997 to 2022, using five-year periods for comparison. Average price and annual production for each period has been added.[27]

Table 9. Average Value of Potash Sales, Revenue to Public, Percentage of Public Share, Volume of Production, and Average Price, 1997–2022[28]

Years	Average Sales per Year (Can$ in billions)	Average Public Share (Can$ in millions)	Average Percentage Public Share (%)[29]	Average Annual Production Volume (Thousand Tonnes)	Average Annual Price (Can$)
1997–2001	1.63	204.92	13.64	8,274.40	196.61
2002–2006	2.09	282.24	13.46	8,896.40	233.01
2007–2011	5.11	618.44	11.25	8,757.76	615.79
2012–2016	5.51	535.55	9.65	10,185.46	480.45
2017–2022	7.96	1,145.77	13.40	13,340.47	612.98

The above information shows that comparing 1997–2001 to 2017–2022, average production by the potash companies increased from 8.1 to 13.3 million tonnes, or about 64 percent. The average price rose from $196.61 to $612.98 per tonne. In real dollar terms, $196.61 in 2019 dollars would be $288.69, meaning a price increase of about 112 percent above inflation.[30] Between 2002–2006 and 2007–2011, production decreased by 2 percent, and price increased by 158 percent. Clearly, increased profits to potash producers after 2007 occurred mainly because world market prices rose, not because of increased investment, assumption of risk, or increased output from the potash companies.

Yet, over time, in both examples above, as high prices yielded higher profits, the public share of potash profits remained about the same, with the benefit of higher prices—all the "windfall"—going to the companies.

The pattern of a stagnant public share, as prices and profits rise, is counter to what should happen in a properly structured economic rent system and represents a shortchanging of the people of Saskatchewan as the resource owners. The amount of the shortfall appears to be in the hundreds of millions of dollars per year for many years and would be in the billions for 2021 and 2022. There is clearly a significant shortfall. The call of various commentators for change seems compelling.

As sales and profits from Saskatchewan potash soared after 2007, the public's share remained stagnant. The windfall should have gone first and foremost to the Saskatchewan public.

The privatization of PCS maximized profit for investors located almost entirely outside of the province. Maximizing return to the resource owners has not been the Saskatchewan government's focus for many years. It is not clear why it would be in the province's interest to see massive amounts of money, far beyond what is required for a healthy investment climate, shipped off to wealthy investors in the United States and elsewhere.

During my twelve years as a member of the provincial cabinet of Saskatchewan, I served as finance minister and industry and resources minister from 1997 to 2007. It was after 2007 that what could be considered windfall profits and larger production really took hold. No trend was apparent until around 2010. This book seeks to shed light on the issue and to demonstrate that, at this juncture, Saskatchewan is asleep at the switch and needs to take measures required to recover a more realistic value for our potash. If and when that happens, the potash companies will have to take time off from laughing all the way to the bank to squawk about how they can't afford to pay any more to Saskatchewan.

According to Nutrien's *Annual Report* 2022, its net sales of potash rose from US$4.04 billion in 2021 to US$7.90 billion in 2022, although the tonnes of potash sold dropped from 13.63 million tonnes in 2021 to 12.54 million tonnes in 2022. Its gross margin for potash sales after cost of goods rose from US$2.75 billion in 2021 to US$6.50 billion in 2022, an increase of US$3.75 billion (Can$4.88 billion).

Nutrien reported payment of provincial mining taxes in the amount of US$1.15 billion in 2022 compared to US$466 million in 2021, an increase of US$683 million (Can$888.65 million).

Of the US$4.88 billion windfall from higher prices Nutrien received in 2022, on top of the windfalls already in place from price increases in previous years, US$888.65 million went to the Province of Saskatchewan, and Nutrien kept US$3.99 billion.

Similarly, according to Mosaic's 10-K filing with the US Securities and Exchange Commission for 2022, its gross margin rose from US$1.06 billion in 2021 based on sales of 7.3 million tonnes of potash to US$2.84 billion, based on sales of 7.2 million tonnes, an increase of 169 percent.

Combining 90 percent of Mosaic's US$1.76 billion increase in gross margin (US$1.61 billion) to take into account its United States production, with Nutrien's additional US$3.75 billion increase, amounts to about

US$5.39 billion—that's the equivalent of about Can$7 billion (at the exchange rate of 0.77 in 2022).

Needless to say, $7 billion is a staggering amount of money. It should be mind-boggling to anyone how this could escape notice. This latest windfall is on top of the excess profits that already existed. Arguably, this entire increase should be going to the owners of the resource, on top of additional amounts from the profit levels through 2021. While the gross margins of Nutrien and Mosaic rose over $7 billion between 2021 and 2022, revenue to government increased from $1.26 billion in 2021 to $2.36 billion in potash taxes and royalties plus the 3 percent resource surcharge on value of sales (about $540 million), for a total of about $2.89 billion in 2022. An increase to the public treasury of about $1.63 billion is close to 23 percent of the windfall for 2022, with 77 percent going to the companies. As will be discussed later in this chapter, the theory of economic rents for extraction of resources is that companies should make a reasonable rate of return on investment and the balance goes to the resource owners. Based on that approach, the Government of Saskatchewan would have taken the entire $7 billion, or $5.4 billion more than it did. A difference of that amount is pretty big. It would be a game-changer for Saskatchewan.

As previously noted, this book deals with the profits the major producers acquire only from potash. That is just part of their revenue, since they have several other divisions, in addition to potash.

The rulers of Saudi Arabia would capture that kind of largesse for themselves. The people of Norway, through their government, would capture it for Norway. Leaving that amount of money, or even half of it, on the table, is depriving the Saskatchewan people of the quality of life and level of revenue they should have. It represents a failure to prepare the province and its people for the best future possible by creating a legacy fund.

These numbers are as hard to fathom as why Saskatchewan is failing to obtain maximum benefit from potash.

They are astonishing.

The value of potash sales, fully set out from government records in appendix A and summarized in Table 1, cannot be compared to the numbers from the companies' annual reports because it involves different sets of figures. The result, however, is the same. Looking at the numbers reported in Saskatchewan government documents, the value of potash sales rose from $7.56 billion in 2021 to $17.98 billion in 2022.[31]

Given the amount of increased revenue and profit the government leaves with the potash companies, it is no surprise that Nutrien noted in its 2022 *Annual Report*: "In 2022, Nutrien delivered record net earnings, due to the strength of agricultural fundamentals, higher fertilizer prices and excellent Nutrien Ag Solutions ("Retail") performance. Our strong cash flow allowed us to invest in the business and return significant cash to our shareholders."[32]

In the technical papers, released with the 2023–2024 Saskatchewan budget, the province projected that potash prices will remain over $742 per tonne until 2027, the end of its forecast period. In addition, it forecasts continued production at current levels. If that proves to be the case, and no changes are made to the tax and royalty system, Saskatchewan will be losing tens of billions of dollars, which could go into provincial coffers and provide a substantial legacy fund.

Curiously, when the potash companies made their then-record sales of $7.56 billion in 2021, the government's take as a percentage of the value of potash sales was 19.24 percent. In 2022, when an even bigger record was set with almost $18 billion, the government's take fell to 16.1 percent.[33] Most people are aware that, as their income increases, and if they become wealthy, the percentage of tax they pay at the higher end goes up. It appears that this is not necessarily the case for the potash companies. Their tax bill may actually drop in percentage terms.

It is hard to imagine how any rational and fair-minded person could regard this state of affairs as anything other than outrageously out of kilter, with no regard to the public interest in obtaining benefit from the value of natural resources.

Between 2008 and 2023, potash producers continued to take increased profits without paying a higher proportion of their income to the province. The annual provincial sales tax paid by Saskatchewan people and businesses was hugely expanded and raised over the same period. The provincial sales tax burden for a family with an income of $75,000 per year doubled from $989 per year in 2008 to $1,932 per year in 2023.[34]

If profits through 2021 were up in the stratosphere, they went into full orbit in 2022. The windfall profit from higher prices rather than from new production is not the first such occurrence. It is built upon pre-existing windfalls and, in that sense, is the tip of the iceberg. Production levels and annual prices for 1997 to 2022 are set out in appendix B.

Combined profits of 2007 for all potash companies were about $1.5 billion, up from about $1 billion in 2006. The price was about the same in both years, and the increased income of 50 percent was due to higher production and sales. The 50 percent increase in profit was earned through greater output from increased effort and spending by the companies.

By contrast, production actually fell from 10.66 million tonnes in 2007 to 9.39 million tonnes in 2008. Profit, however, soared from $1.48 billion in 2007 to $4.48 billion in 2008. The increased profit was due to the fact the potash price went from $286 per tonne in 2007 to $746 per tonne in 2008. It did not result from extra effort or spending on the companies' part. The potash simply went up in price.

The higher price in 2008 resulted in a $3 billion increase in gross profit. Government revenue rose from $524.47 million to $1.59 billion, an increase of $1.06 billion. The industry took the other $2 billion of the windfall. It is interesting that the government increase in 2008 was $1.06 billion out of $3 billion. In 2022, the additional revenue was $1.6 billion out of $7 billion in additional gross profit.[35] In both cases, and in other years, increased value for potash benefitted companies much more than the public.

In 2007, the potash companies made higher profits than they had ever achieved,[36] at a price of $286.71 per tonne.[37] If we considered that price as a base price for future years, which would allow them to make a reasonable profit, with additional revenue from higher price minus increased costs viewed as windfall profits, the result would be that the companies would be entitled to keep the amounts from the first column in table 10 below. The second column is the average price per year, which is more reflective of the revenue they actually received. The difference between the two numbers amounts to a windfall for the companies.

Table 10. 2007 Base Price Adjusted for Inflation and Actual Price, 2007–2022

Year	2007 Price in Real Dollar Terms (in Can$ per metric tonne)	Actual Price (in Can$ per metric tonne)
2007	286.71	286.71
2008	291.91	746.54
2009	296.08	809.03
2010	300.76	569.74

Table 10. (continued)

Year	2007 Price in Real Dollar Terms (in Can$ per metric tonne)	Actual Price (in Can$ per metric tonne)
2011	307.26	666.95
2012	315.33	583.53
2013	319.23	486.12
2014	322.87	575.44
2015	326.26	373.19
2016	330.68	383.96
2017	337.44	440.97
2018	344.73	457.00
2019	349.93	490.00
2020	357.48	387.31
2021	361.38	567.80
2022	381.93	1,334.80

Admittedly, this is just a rough indication of what might be considered a good starting point to examine what the windfall profits of the potash companies amount to. If a different index for adjusting the base price of potash is a more accurate one, that index could be adopted. The concept of a base price adjusted for inflation, however, would still be appropriate. This rough approach doesn't take into account the fact that there are increased production costs within the numbers that are unknown, and adjustments to account for that and perhaps other matters need to be considered. The system of collecting taxes and royalties for potash should take fluctuations of price, up or down, into account and should inherently take profit level into account. The problem is that Saskatchewan doesn't have a system of taxation and royalties that takes those basic factors into account and can be seen to operate rationally according to understandable factors. Once the prices took off and demand soared after 2007, the system did not work anymore. It needed to be adjusted. The government has tinkered with the system a bit in those years, but not in a way that fixes this basic problem. The province has already lost billions of dollars that should have been used for some basic needs, as will be discussed in chapter 11.

It seems fair to factor in a price at which a reasonable rate of return for investment is still being earned, and that should happen using the 2007 price adjusted for inflation, since the 2007 price was quite a bit higher than the price had ever been prior to 2006. The price had been in the $100 to $200 range until 2004 when it went up to $216.82. In 2006, it hit $296.16 and then was slightly lower in 2007 at $286.71 level. Then it exploded and ever since then has ranged between $383.96 and the 2022 jackpot of an average $1,334.80.

The price, to state the obvious, is a good indicator of the value of potash, and the public, as owner, should have a system in place to recover the value of the product they are selling. It is no different than oil companies or oil and gas retailers altering their prices as the applicable market price goes up and down, or wholesalers or retailers of bananas, oranges, or cauliflower passing on varying market prices to the consumer. You don't see other retailers charging the same price for fifteen years while the value of their commodity doubles. And you don't see potash companies entering into supply agreements that guarantee a low price for potash for decades at a time. So why would a province do so in the case of its most valuable resource?

In 2007, the potash companies made money when the price was $286.71 per tonne. The PCS 2007 *Annual Report* states that the company was left "in a very strong financial position" and aimed to "put [its] strengths—and cash—to work for [its] investors, building an even stronger company for tomorrow."[38] CFO Wayne Brownlee stated: "Our potash potential is tremendous, with higher demand and prices."[39] Noting that in 2007 potash was, as it had always been, the company's "biggest earnings contributor,"[40] the report stated that PCS was "a thriving international fertilizer enterprise—the global leader in potash."[41]

So just using PCS as an example, the companies were doing very well when the price was $286.71 per tonne. They were very strong financially and thriving.

To the extent the current price exceeds the 2007 base price adjusted for inflation (minus increased production costs), the revenue over and above that amount is of a windfall nature since it simply results from higher prices. The price went from $286.71 per tonne in 2007 to $746.54 in 2008 before settling down to the $500 to $600 range in the years that followed.

Taking the base price adjusted for inflation and comparing it to the average price, which could have been received in subsequent years, results in additional price per tonne and, therefore, represents a windfall. Looking only at the average price per year is not completely accurate because, as already stated, the companies might not sell all the potash produced in the same specific year, and they would be subject to longer term supply contracts. So, if we took into account that stockpiling and contracts might prevent them from getting the higher price for all sales each year, the higher price would still have a dramatic impact because most of the sales would be at the higher price. For this analysis, the yearly average price is stated along with the base price plus inflation to give an idea of the range in which windfall revenue would be. It would not actually be as high as the maximum, but at least the maximum possible would define the top of the range. From the windfall revenue, deductions would be made for increased production costs. With that qualifier, essentially what this exercise does is present the general nature of windfall profits that have been left largely to the companies since 2008 and which I argue belong to the people of the province and should be collected, at least on a go-forward basis.

Table 11 illustrates a calculation of the potential range of windfall profits. It provides an illustration of the maximum potential windfall revenue. This figure is based upon the assumption that all tonnes produced per year were sold at the average price per tonne per year. This assumption is not exact as not all the tonnes produced would be sold in the same year and not all would be sold at the average yearly price because of longer-term supply contracts. As well, revenue to government from the industry each year would have to be examined to determine whether the amount of annual revenue was such that the windfall profit could be offset by or against revenue government received to some extent, in a taxation and royalty system, which could be understood and predictable in terms of its relationship to price and profit level. We should bear in mind those qualifiers as we examine table 11, which illustrates an order of magnitude in the revenue levels Saskatchewan may be foregoing by not capturing windfall profits.

Table 11 is not meant to suggest that the Government of Saskatchewan should collect additional taxes and royalties from 2008. Those years are done. It is meant to inform the discussion of what should occur going forward.

Table 11 suggests a posible shortfall of up to $38.8 billion for 2008–2022. To put this in context, table 7 demonstrates that the gross profit from the potash divisions of the companies in that period was over $50 billion.

Table 11. Method to Illustrate Potential Windfall Profits, 2008–2022[42]

Year	2007 Base Price in Real Dollars	Average Price per Tonne (Can$)	Potential Windfall per Tonne ($)	Tonnes Produced (in thousands)	Maximum Annual Windfall Revenue (in Can$ billions)*
2008	291.91	746.54	454.63	9,390.4	4.27
2009	296.08	809.03	512.95	4,250.6	2.18
2010	300.76	569.74	268.98	9,108.5	2.45
2011	307.26	666.95	359.69	10,377.9	3.73
2012	315.33	583.53	268.20	8,825.5	2.37
2013	319.27	486.12	166.85	9,737.5	1.62
2014	322.87	575.44	252.57	10,273.5	2.59
2015	326.26	373.19	46.93	11,124.7	0.52
2016	330.68	383.96	53.28	10,966.1	0.58
2017	337.44	440.97	103.53	12,407.4	1.28
2018	344.73	457.00	112.27	11,743.2	1.32
2019	349.93	490.00	140.07	10,659.1	1.49
2020	357.48	387.31	29.83	12,122.4	0.36
2021	361.38	567.80	206.42	12,241.8	2.53
2022	381.93	1,334.80	952.87	12,354.9	11.77

* *Potential Windfall per Tonne times Tonnes Produced equals Annual Windfall Revenue.*

Since the taxation and royalty system is not properly adjusted according to profit level, although the amount of the shortfall represented in table 11 may seem to be high, so have the profits of the companies been very high. During the years in question, profits from potash averaged about $3.5 billion per year. Table 11, while not necessarily an exact description of windfall profits not taken by the province, would represent an average maximum of about $2.6 billion per year that the government left on the table. Of course, the numbers in any given year would vary quite a bit from those figures. In 2008, for example, when the price jumped dramatically and the industry had a $3 billion windfall, in an economic rent system, that $3 billion would go to the public treasury. Table 11 illustrates a shortfall of $2.72 billion in 2008—a scenario that is conceivable.

The bottom line is that, in most years, the government should have captured hundreds of millions of dollars more, and in certain years, billions more. The companies may justifiably challenge the numbers presented in table 11 or the suggested methodology. That's only reasonable, and if another set of numbers or another method is developed or more accurate, it can be used instead. This may never occur with respect to past years since no one is suggesting going back; however, a new model to calculate windfall profits and the public's share can be implemented for the future.

Lest anyone think that I have just figured all this out all by myself, others were way ahead of me. Alarm bells were sounded. But nobody seems to be paying much attention.

Voices on the left, such as that of economist and former MP Erin Weir, have produced work to demonstrate taxes and royalties the potash companies paid are too low.

The imbalance between profit for the potash companies and return to the people of the province is not, however, something only those on the left notice.

Jack Mintz of the University of Calgary's School of Public Policy has spoken and written several times since 2010 about problems with the Saskatchewan potash royalty structure. In a 2010 report for the Conference Board of Canada, he argued that the province's royalty structure was a complex mess, resulting from Liberal, NDP, and Progressive Conservative governments of Saskatchewan. In 2015, Mintz wrote: "The first step is to simplify the potash profit tax to mimic other systems that apply a simple tax rate to 'economic rents' (revenues net of current and capital costs)....If prices go up, Saskatchewan will get a fair share of rents and, if prices go down, producers won't face onerous taxation levels."[43]

Mintz also proposed a minimum tax so the province always had some stable revenue during downturns, which would be creditable against future profit tax. His proposals in that regard are attractive because revenue to government would be tied to profit. The problem Saskatchewan has is that, as profits have increased, the public's share has decreased or remained stagnant. The opposite should occur. As profit becomes much larger, the concept of economic rent is that the proportion to government from those profits also should be greater. Mintz's proposal would fix that problem and would be a welcome and needed change.[44]

In a 2015 opinion piece in the *Financial Post*, Mintz praised the 2015 Saskatchewan budget, because it promised a potash tax review.[45] That review has never taken place. After all, according to the industry, there is no need for a review or any change.

Speaking in Saskatchewan about a report he authored in 2015 with Duanjie Chen, Jack Mintz repeated their call for an overhaul of Saskatchewan's potash royalty and tax structure, a call he and Chen had made in a previous (2013) report. Speaking about the report, he stated that between 2009 and 2015, the province lost revenues of $2.4 billion because of its failure to collect economic rents.[46] That's over $300 million per year.

In their 2015 report, "Potash Taxation: How Canada's Regime Is Neither Efficient nor Competitive from an International Perspective," Mintz and Chen call for a rent-based royalty system that taxes revenue net of capital spending and operational costs.[47] The report suggested that Saskatchewan's current approach represented a failure to collect billions in extra revenue and that a rent-based tax system was required, especially to ensure a fair provincial return during boom times.

Mintz and Chen compare the "marginal effective tax rate" for potash companies in Saskatchewan to seven other countries where potash mining takes place. Combining all forms of taxes paid in each place, they range between 13.9 percent in Belarus to 21.9 percent in Germany, with China, Jordan, Israel, Russia, and the United States in between these figures, all between 16.1 percent and 21.6 percent. For Saskatchewan, the rate could be as high as 22.6 percent, but could also be as low as 0.3 percent.[48]

In their 2013 report, Mintz and Chen compared the marginal effective tax rate charged to the potash companies with the same rate as applied to other sectors of the Saskatchewan economy. The 2013 study sets out the marginal effective tax rate as described in table 12 below.[49]

Table 12. Marginal Effective Tax Rates for Sectors of the Saskatchewan Economy

Sector	Tax Rate
Oil and Gas	37.1
Communications	35.5
Construction	31.9
Other Services	31.1
Wholesale Trade	28.7
Retail Trade	28.0
Transportation and Storage	23.2
Electrical Power, Gas, and Water	22.6
Potash	-0.4 to 21.9
Agriculture	21.9
Manufacturing	17.7
Forestry	16.1
Metallic Mining	11.0

Why is the richest and most powerful industry in the province, owned almost entirely by shareholders outside of Saskatchewan, given a lower tax rate than people in Saskatchewan who own construction companies? Why are they favoured over a mom-and-pop who own a retail establishment? Why do they pay less than people who own hotels? Why do they get a break that trucking companies don't get? Or people working in communications?

The returns to the potash companies have been growing enormously as we have seen. Understandably, when the industry was beginning some sixty years ago, it needed consideration, because the companies were making big investments and not making very big returns. It is also understandable that when the potash price was a fraction of what it had been for the last fifteen years and the government wanted the mines refurbished and new mines built, it might extend a tax incentive to investors to build infrastructure costing tens of billions of dollars. But it is not understandable why this special treatment should apply under circumstances that have now existed for a decade and a half.

As a former finance minister, I know that putting together a budget involves many decisions. There are choices as to how you tax individuals, small businesses, large corporations, and different sectors of the economy. There are choices about how you spend money. For example, should the priority be education to support young people for the future? Do seniors need help? What about the health care system? You make decisions to give people a tax break sometimes or decide maybe that others should pay more. You make decisions to spend in an area that benefits a particular group. Maybe it's the working poor with children. Or the middle class or seniors. One thing always factors into the equation: if you decide that some pay less, others pay more. If you give more to some, you give less to others.

When government decides that the mining companies, for some reason, should get the lion's share of Saskatchewan's wealth from potash, they are not doing something that makes the province business-friendly and keeps the economy going. On the contrary, the decision is not business-friendly because it favours one sector and, inevitably, that means other sectors pay more. It also means that government must make choices on the spending side that can hurt people because the resources available to government to do its job helping society are not there to the extent they should be.

It also means that ordinary people are paying tax rates that are higher than they should be. That's why it is relevant to point out, as previously mentioned, that while the potash companies ramped up their wealth since 2007, Saskatchewan families had their sales tax burden doubled because the government needed money. It is hard to understand why an industry that effectively can only operate in the province of Saskatchewan would be favoured over industries and individuals that can do business or live in another place.

The government's management of the potash resource should be examined in the context of other sectors of the economy to determine whether there is a balanced approach. The favourable tax treatment given to the most profitable and non-mobile industry in the province has not been the subject of much public discussion in Saskatchewan. As Mintz and Chen put it, "The potash sector is taxed relatively lightly for marginal investments compared to a broad range of industries."[50] They conclude that reform of the fiscal regime for potash "is in the public interest of all residents of Saskatchewan."[51]

Notwithstanding that it was apparent prices and profits were soaring and the province's proportionate share was not increasing, and notwithstanding objective and expert assessment, including that from Mintz and Chen, advising the government that since 2009 the people of the province were losing billions of dollars, Premier Brad Wall responded to the report by saying the province got a "pretty good return."[52]

There was at least one potash expert who agreed with Wall. While I like to think I got along with Saskatchewan's business community fairly well, I have to admit that Bill Doyle was much happier dealing with Wall than he was with Roy Romanow or me. When he retired in 2014 after fifteen years as PCS president and CEO, he and his family owned US$308 million in PCS shares and stock options worth US$192 million, as well as additional retirement payments. In 2010, his accumulated wealth from PCS salary, bonuses, pensions, and stock options was estimated by *Forbes* magazine to be US$500 million.[53] His accumulated wealth at retirement would exceed the total royalties and taxes paid to the million-plus people of Saskatchewan in all but a few of the years in the almost forty years of PCS mining potash.

In 2015, in response to the report by Chen and Mintz, Wall again reiterated that no change was needed to the tax and royalty system for potash. He based his conclusion on the fact that BHP was building a $12 billion mine and so determined that the tax system "seems to be working pretty good for the province's economy."[54] This is a bit of a non sequitur. The fact that BHP is proceeding is not necessarily evidence that the tax and royalty system is fair to the citizens of the province. Upon retirement, Doyle stated that he felt Wall's government represented "the first time" government understood that "Saskatchewan is truly a great place. It has exceptionally smart entrepreneurial people who work hard. And we are fortunate that we now have a government that understands how government should operate to encourage investment." He added that Wall would be "a good prime minister for Canada."[55]

It's good to get along with others. Still, I'm not sure it's a good thing when big business doesn't have any complaints about the government or politicians in power. The job of business is to push the envelope forward to maximize value for shareholders or owners. Government's job is to promote the public interest and to push the envelope back to maintain a fair balance. If industry feels it has everything it wants, and government is doing a good job from the point of view of business, can it be assumed that the public interest has been kept front and centre in the relationship between government and big business?

A few years after Doyle retired, in 2017, another report would come out, this time by Jim Marshall of the University of Regina/University of Saskatchewan Johnson Shoyama Graduate School of Public Policy. The report concluded the province has lost its historical share of potash profit, and "it would seem that any review of potash taxes in Saskatchewan could be expected to result in a greater share of the proceeds from potash flowing to the people of Saskatchewan through royalties and taxes than has been the case in recent years, as opposed to a shift in the split towards the producing companies."[56]

Erin Weir had authored opinion pieces in the *Regina Leader-Post* and *Saskatoon StarPhoenix* as early as 2010 and 2011 to the same effect. In addition to citing other examples already mentioned, Weir encapsulated the imbalance between profit and return to the province in one specific year:

> The potash industry extracted the same tonnage from Saskatchewan in 2005 and 2008. Entirely due to price increases, this output was worth $4.7 billion more in 2008 than in 2005.
>
> Most of this gain should have accrued to the people of Saskatchewan, who own the resource. Yet provincial potash royalties rose by only $1.1 billion between the 2005 and 2008 fiscal years.[57]

Again, the public share in the form of royalties rose by $1.1 billion, while $3.6 billion in increased revenue went to big business and external shareholders. No questions are asked by the government or media commentators. There is no indication the government sees any need for change.

In 2022, as previously noted, the increase was about $10 billion over 2021, of which the government took in about $1.6 billion, or 16 percent, leaving 84 percent to the industry.

As the Mintz and Chen studies of 2013 and 2015 point out, the potash tax and royalty system is very complex and not responsive to price and profit increases or decreases. Therefore, results such as those cited occur and underline the absurdity of the potash tax and royalty system. As they put it: "A royalty regime should assess the rents earned by the industry—rents being the surplus in excess of the cost of exploration, development, and extraction."[58] Mintz and Chen explain that a royalty and tax system should result in greater return to the province by capturing profits that exceed costs and a reasonable return on investment.

What would be a "reasonable return" for the potash companies? Mintz and Chen assert:

> In the context of resource industries, fairness could be assessed in terms of the "fair share" taken by the government, as owner of the resource, in rents across different resource industries (e.g., potash, metallic mining, and oil and gas). In principle, the government, as owner of the resource, should receive 100 percent of the rents. However, to invite private producers to explore, develop, and extract resources, the government must offer a competitive return...to attract investors.[59]

The authors state "an efficient tax structure is marked by neutrality," declaring that the tax system should result in a similar level of tax between industries, and thereby avoid distorting investment and production decisions.[60] They point out that the burden of provincial taxes in Saskatchewan for potash companies, by far the most profitable companies in the province, even at its highest level, is below the midpoint among other resource industries (such as metallic mining, and oil and gas) and non-resource industries. In some circumstances, its burden in recent years is substantially below the marginal effective tax rate (METR).

When the NDP opposition suggested in 2019 that the review promised in the 2015 budget might be a good idea, the potash companies said there was no need to review Saskatchewan's "very, very successful" taxation and royalty regime. They were "relatively happy with the present tax system."[61]

Faced with outside analysts from the left, right, and centre saying the public is being quite substantially shortchanged, and industry executives saying things are fine as they are, the government must have considered whether there was a problem to be addressed. It apparently was confident in the advice it was receiving from the experts at the potash companies.

Normally, the business sector sees the need to press the envelope forward for lower taxes, which they claim will result in economic development and jobs. Rarely does big business say things are fine the way they are. When big business says that everything is right, it would be wise to listen to their views, and at the same time, to listen to the views of independent experts and analysts to ensure the interests of the broader community were thoroughly considered, in addition to the interests of the business sector.

FIXING THE POTASH TAX PROBLEM

CCORDING TO THE SASKATCHEWAN MINING ASSOCIATION'S "Saskatchewan Potash Report for 2020,"[1] Saskatchewan potash companies invest in community initiatives, programs, and causes that enhance quality of life across the province, investing $10.5 million in various communities and Indigenous partnerships that year. Given the projected gross profits of about $1.85 billion from potash operations in 2020, $10.5 million—about 0.5 percent of the companies' profit from potash—would appear to be affordable.

According to the Mosaic website Time to Dig Deeper, in 2017, potash producers donated $15.5 million in community investment.

That same year (PCS's last year of operation prior to merging with Nutrien), it was reported that PCS was likely the largest corporate donor in Saskatoon and that, since 2010, the company had spent US$134 million in "community investment."[2]

Nutrien and Mosaic, like PCS, are highly visible as sponsors of major cultural and recreational venues. Various recreation sites and sports venues, including the home of the Saskatchewan Roughriders, are named for their corporate sponsors.

From 2010 to 2017, PCS made gross profits from its Saskatchewan potash operations of close to US$11 billion.[3] If community investment at close to 1 percent of profit creates enough goodwill that Saskatchewan continues to allow the potash companies to take billions of dollars, which should belong to the people of the province, then it surely must be the best investment potash producers ever made.

Such donations are needed and welcome. They will be as long as government revenue and expenditure is such that the community needs to raise funds for vital services for people, such as state-of-the-art hospital equipment, women's shelters, assistance to those reliant on social assistance rates below the poverty line, food banks, soup kitchens, and public parks, to name some services where corporate sponsorship can play a key role.

Corporate donations create goodwill in the community. A good image, enhanced through corporate sponsorship, may reduce the likelihood of questions being raised about whether corporate giants are paying their fair share into public coffers.

Greater Saskatoon Chamber of Commerce CEO Jason Aebig noted that "resource extraction companies were sensitive to communities in which they operated because of a perception that natural resources belong to the people who live on them."[4] In this case, perception, for a change, turns out to be reality. The natural resources do, for the most part, belong to the people of the province. They don't belong to mining companies. The public is entitled to monitor the appropriate level of return as circumstances evolve. For that matter, other industries and ordinary taxpayers may benefit from potash tax reform. Resource companies should be extremely sensitive to communities from which great wealth is derived.

In 2016, the top six senior managers at PCS were paid about $17.2 million, roughly equivalent to the average amount of community investments PCS made yearly from 2010 to 2017.[5]

Not much that potash companies or executives do seems to attract critical scrutiny. In 2022, when Russia's war on Ukraine created shortages that drove up commodity prices, including potash and fuel, inflation kicked in and the cost of food rose rapidly and noticeably, causing problems for many families. Politicians blamed the grocery chains, including Loblaws and Sobeys. Federal NDP leader Jagmeet Singh called for a windfall profit tax on big food retailers, and insisted Galen Weston Jr., the CEO of Loblaws, be called before the House of Commons Standing Committee on Agriculture and Agri-Food to answer questions about profiteering.

Along with Michael Medline, the CEO of Empire Company (Sobeys), Weston Jr. appeared and stated that although his company made large profits in its diversified operations, which include more than food, the profit on food was one dollar for every twenty-five dollars of food sold. This has not been challenged, and the Loblaws CEO felt it was not unreasonable and did not represent excessive profiteering. He explained that the food retailers were simply passing on higher costs they incurred for things such as transportation and the cost of food itself, since inputs such as fertilizer and fuel had gone up in price.

In an *Edmonton Journal* article about the committee hearing, Sylvain Charlebois, an expert on food prices who regularly appears in the national media, is quoted as saying the profit on food at the retail end is small, and the price increases are due to higher fuel and other costs the grocers pay and pass on to the consumer.[6]

So what has this got to do with the profits of Saskatchewan's potash mining companies? In going after Galen Weston Jr. and Loblaws, politicians are looking in the wrong place and, once again, paying no attention to where the big profits are being taken. Loblaws made the same profit in 2022 as in 2021, according to Weston Jr.[7] It did not benefit from inflation in food prices. One of the important costs in food production is the cost of fertilizer. Nutrien is the largest fertilizer company in the world, and Mosaic is a large fertilizer-producing company as well. In Nutrien's case, its gross profit more than doubled from 2021 to 2022: its after-tax earnings went from US$3.2 billion in 2021 to almost US$7.7 billion in 2022.[8]

Weir mentions the controversy surrounding the Loblaws CEO's pay increasing from $11 million in 2021 to $12 million in 2022, pointing out that "there has not been the same media or political interest in Nutrien paying its former CEO the equivalent of $23 million in one year."[9]

This is par for the course when it comes to the hands-off treatment potash mining companies seem to get. Weir noted the US$3.7 billion increase to Nutrien profits in 2022 over 2021, highlighting that "only 18 percent of this potash windfall went to the citizens who supposedly own the potash."[10] Weir points out that this is indicative of the entire potash industry. "We would be far better served by royalty and tax policies to collect the windfall profits these higher prices create on our natural resource," he concluded.[11]

We are not going to get too far taxing the windfall profits of Loblaws, or Galen Weston Jr.'s million-dollar raise. When you start talking about the billions being left on the table for the shareholders of the potash companies, then we are getting somewhere.

This side story about Loblaws and other grocers is relevant because it underscores the point that, although potash mining windfall profits have been in place for a decade and a half, occur in broad daylight, and are duly noted by experts, they remain ignored by government and the media. Accordingly, they are unknown to the general public, and not a topic of concern. The public relies, in this sense, on elected representatives to ensure its interests are being attended to. The potash companies seem to be exempt from scrutiny and from the concept that everyone should pay their fair share, which should be determined largely by the ability to pay and the expectation that the wealthiest among us can contribute. Of course, we may be reminded of the jobs the companies bring to the province, not to mention charitable donations.

Everyone would agree that employment in the mining sector is very important to Saskatchewan and that whatever charity the companies can offer to the people of the province is welcome too. According to the Saskatchewan Mining Association, the potash sector employed 5,400 workers directly in Saskatchewan in 2021, with total annual salaries of $784 million.[12]

A payroll of $784 million is big and impressive. To put it in context, compare it to the profits mining companies made from Saskatchewan potash, which in 2021 amounted to about $4.6 billion. In 2022, that figure was $11.8 billion. A payroll of close to $800 million does not justify failing to tax the profits from potash.

Potash companies do benefit Saskatchewan in many ways—as employers, purchasers of goods and services, taxpayers, and charitable supporters. Appreciating those efforts does not mean we can't ask if current contributions are in sync with the ability to pay, relative to other taxpayers and the needs of Saskatchewan people. As corporate citizens in the places where they mine, resource companies should pay their share of taxes as well as contribute to the community in other ways, just as citizens do generally.

It is easier to identify the place where most of the profits do not end up—Saskatchewan—than to see exactly where they flow, because the potash companies are traded on the stock market. There is no public list of shareholders, and the list changes on an ongoing basis.

The profits from Saskatchewan potash mines flow outside the province, largely to investment funds owning millions of shares. While some of those investment funds may manage money on behalf of many others, including the people of Saskatchewan, the amount of PCS or Nutrien or Mosaic shares the people of Saskatchewan owned would be very small.

As discussed previously, Weir estimates that Saskatchewan lost $18 to $36 billion due to the privatization of PCS as of 2010, the year of his study. This amounts to about $857 million to $1.7 billion per year.[13] As also previously discussed, one doesn't have to advocate public ownership to assert that the province is not receiving its fair share of profits from the publicly traded potash companies. Without considering losses from privatization, Jack Mintz estimated Saskatchewan lost $2.4 billion in royalties by its failure to capture a greater share of increased profits between 2009 and 2015, an average of well over $300 million per year. Jim Marshall of the Johnson Shoyama Graduate School of Public Policy speculated the province has been giving up $40 to $100 million per year since 2009 by failing to secure the public share of higher profits from potash.

Earlier, it was mentioned that the gross profits from potash in the last few years have been very high. That was true even in 2019. The impact of high prices on the potash companies' gross profits is reflected in Nutrien's *2019 Annual Report*, which cites the following facts: 73 percent gross margin per manufactured tonne (excluding depreciation and amortization) and $63 potash cash cost of product manufactured per tonne.[14]

In 2019, Nutrien could produce a ton of potash for US$63 (Can$83.60), about Can$75.24 per metric tonne, while the average price of a metric tonne in 2019 was Can$490. In 2021 and 2022, the average price was $567.80 and $1,334.80 respectively, which is why the gross profit of Nutrien from potash in those years was 68.35 percent and 86.3 percent respectively. As well, half of the last fifteen years have been even more profitable for Nutrien or its predecessors, PCS and Agrium.

Mintz, now President's Fellow at the University of Calgary School of Public Policy,[15] is one of the leading tax economists in the world. He has repeatedly pointed out what is needed: a system that charges royalties and taxes based on profit and that ensures the lion's share of profits over and above a reasonable return on investment goes to the resource owner. It is difficult to imagine anything simpler and more reasonable than that. It is difficult to understand why public policy-makers have refused to do so. The amounts involved are staggering. The issues facing the province, as will be discussed in the next chapter, are daunting. Additional funds available to the government could substantially resolve some of the serious issues the province is facing. Rather than just having tax cuts or programs for affluent people or agribusiness, Saskatchewan could have government policy to combat poverty and deficiencies in the education and health sectors. Saskatchewan must decide if the well-being of untold numbers of residents, present and future, is more important than the well-being of affluent external shareholders. For some time, the shareholders and corporate executives have been winning out.

Saskatchewan has everything going for it in terms of its ability to leverage its incredible potash resource for the benefit of the people of the province. It was already established in the 1970s that this can be done. If the government or the public cannot embrace the notion of some public ownership of a part of the industry as a means of keeping more of the profits at home, surely the taxation levers that the province has should be used to do so. Why on earth would the province hesitate?

The solution is not difficult. As profits rise, the public's share should rise exponentially. It hasn't. Precisely what a reasonable split is, and what a fair return to the companies would be, can be examined by qualified and objective people provided with information on the costs of potash extraction. This way, the public could be advised whether they are receiving a price reflecting the value of their resource.

It may be argued that the resource sector is volatile, and profits rise and fall with the markets. That's true. As Chen and Mintz point out, however, that simply means you build into the tax and royalty system a cushion to protect government revenue stability, and a system to bring the producers to a proper profit level where the cushioning has resulted in a temporary overpayment to government.[16] As well, larger returns to government in some years can be partially set aside in a stabilization fund to provide needed funds in the event of a downturn.

Can the potash companies afford to pay a lot more to the people of Saskatchewan and still make good profits? Surely, there can be no doubt. At present, the shortfall is in the billions of dollars.

CORPORATE WINDFALL, SASKATCHEWAN SHORTFALL

WHAT DIFFERENCE DOES A TAX AND ROYALTY SYSTEM FOR POT-
ash make to the people of Saskatchewan? What would be different under a system that acquired maximum value from the potash resource for the public?

Everything.

The Saskatchewan budgets for 2007 and 2022 projected public debt levels of $7.3 billion and $19.5 billion, respectively. The level of public debt, while not the worst in Canada as a percentage of GDP or on a per capita basis, more than doubled as potash producers accrued windfall profits. So in addition to their sales tax burden doubling as the potash companies took their profits, the people of Saskatchewan also saw their debt burden double.

Notwithstanding record economic growth, the Saskatchewan Party ran deficit budgets for most years between 2007 and 2022. Deficit budgets and increasing public debt have consequences for people as governments seek to take corrective measures to change budget trend lines to make spending more closely match revenue and reverse the trend of rising public debt.

Ironically, the trickle-down theory, that rewarding the wealthy will result in benefits for lower-income people as money released into the economy generates economic activity, probably works in reverse when it comes to the treatment of potash companies. Since the profits flow outside of the province, if the money does generate economic activity, there's no reason to think the activity will necessarily be in Saskatchewan. Some of it will, because if the potash companies prosper, they will invest in refurbishing and expanding potash mines as they have done so. At some point, however, there's no more room for expansion and refurbishment and most of the profits simply enrich shareholders in other places. To the extent they may trickle down, they trickle down on people elsewhere.

Erin Weir's estimate that privatization cost the province between $18 billion and $38 billion between 1989 and 2010, even taking the lowest projection, amounts to about $1 billion a year. It is not hyperbole to state that if Saskatchewan had received that revenue, it would be a much different place. We don't need to consider what can happen if a jurisdiction decides to control part of the natural resource sector for public benefit. It's not a pie-in-the-sky scenario. It's been done in Norway with its half of one percent of the world's oil reserves. That country has used its resource wealth to benefit its current population and leave a legacy for the future. Saudi Arabia has also captured wealth from its oil, although without a commitment to equitable distribution of wealth, such as Norway adheres to. Greater benefit to the province of Saskatchewan occurred in the 1970s through public ownership, as the Economic Council of Canada study cited earlier concluded, and as even the conservative Frontier Centre study also conceded was likely the case for the people of Saskatchewan.

Perhaps even in a place that has elected social democratic governments before, a preference for private development will continue to preclude government from having a mandate to invest in and take ownership of part of the resource sector. Even in that circumstance, the vast majority of the public would probably agree that government should still maximize return to the people of the province, while ensuring the private sector earns a reasonable return on investment.

While this book's purpose is not to presume to set out the precise amount that should be collected, or what a reasonable return on investment for the companies would amount to, voices from the left, right, and centre have all identified a significant problem with Saskatchewan's current approach. The numbers involved are large and the evidence compelling. The fact of rising profits without exponentially increasing the government's revenue is apparent from the companies' own reports. It's not unreasonable to state the province has been leaving hundreds of millions of dollars per year—and, in some cases, billions per year—on the table.

Leaving that money on the table while, until recently, running deficits year after year results in government either looking for increased revenue from other sources or cutting benefits to people, or both.

The 2017 Saskatchewan budget raised the provincial sales tax from 5 percent to 6 percent and expanded it to other goods and services to bring in an additional approximately $900 million per year from Saskatchewan residents and businesses. Since then, further expansions in the sales tax base have been implemented. While potash companies' taxes were also increased in the 2017 budget by over $100 million per year, the new sales tax levies dwarfed that adjustment. Taxing average families for purchasing children's clothing or fast food, coupled with cutting or freezing benefits for the most disadvantaged members of society, have been regarded as the primary way to make a correction. Significantly increased revenue from multinational corporations earning windfall profits in an industry that is most profitably pursued in Saskatchewan has not been the approach taken. The government could easily and profitably operate the potash industry if shut down by the private sector. That's already been demonstrated.

Decisions that benefit the few can have consequences for many. As Saskatchewan's minister of finance from 1997 to 2003, I learned that most of the time you don't have very much discretion over distribution of public funds. In theory, you can decide everything. In practice, you quickly learn that public health care will take 40 cents of every dollar the province receives, and education will take more than 20 cents. Basically, those two items will take two-thirds of the usual available revenue. You're not going to make significant cuts to health care or education. They are indispensable public investments. Then you have social assistance, highways, interest on the public debt, funding to municipalities, support for agriculture through expenditure or tax exemptions, and a variety of other areas of government spending demanded by the public and the representatives they send to the legislative assembly. You can tinker a bit, and sometimes reform the tax system, but in terms of additional spending on social programs, there often isn't any left over. In fact, governments often have little flexibility after simply maintaining the programs and services they oversee, and often operate in the red just doing that.

Even on a multi-billion-dollar budget, if you have $50 million to do something with by the time the treasury board has finished its review of the departments' spending plans, you're lucky.

Other ministers and their deputies start clamouring to get some of it, so getting agreement on what to do isn't easy.

Could the government of Saskatchewan make good use of increased revenue?

In its 2017 budget, in addition to levying increased consumption taxes, the government of Saskatchewan made some choices impacting low-income people. Social assistance was cut by removing funding of school supplies for kids whose families are on welfare. A program to assist the working poor by providing income supplements to ensure they made as much as they would on welfare and cover their medical costs was cut by removing funding for kids over the age of thirteen. Education was cut by 6.7 percent. Exactly how people on welfare are supposed to cover school supplies was not explained. At the same time, a fine options program that allowed low-income people to work off fines through community service was cut, along with an Indigenous court worker program. How sending more people to jail would save public funds was not explained. Meanwhile, high-income people were given a five percent reduction on their personal income taxes. As a fully employed mining company executive, my taxes went down by $4,000 per year as a result. That money was not needed and did not go to investment in Saskatchewan. It simply was added to an investment portfolio.

Saskatchewan continues to have the lowest minimum wage in Canada. Indigenous students in on-reserve K-12 schools continue to receive education funding at a rate of 50 percent per student compared to off-reserve schools. Support for the elderly in long-term care homes has been repeatedly shown to be inadequate due to lack of staffing. People often go without prescription medicine because of the cost involved, and more support would be welcome and increase quality of life, while likely reducing emergency room and hospital visits and stays. Homelessness is on the rise and investment in public housing and other supports could make a difference. Educational assistance for special needs children is reduced year after year. Post-secondary education funding has been reduced in several years and at best is frozen.

Another casualty of the 2017 Saskatchewan budget was the Saskatchewan Transportation Company (STC). STC was a long-standing government-owned bus company. It provided intercity transportation to elderly people who could no longer drive and to people in rural and northern areas unable to afford their own vehicles. Many people depended upon the service to allow them to continue to live in small towns and remote areas, to get to medical appointments in the city, to shop, or to visit. Farmers obtained needed parts in a timely way through STC's express parcel service. The rationale for ending the bus service was that it "lost" $14 million per year. Saskatchewan budgeted over $600 million for transportation spending in its 2021–2022 budget. The bulk of that is spent on highways. That expenditure is not considered a "loss." In that context, it is questionable whether expenditure on bus service for people without vehicles should be seen simply as a loss.

The private sector also shut down bus service throughout most of Canada. But the government is not the private sector. Sometimes a need that cannot be effectively met by the private sector should still be met by the public sector. Government is about service to people, not about profit.

Investing in education and skills training is how successful societies enable people to achieve their potential and put food on the table. Such spending results in more productive, healthy individuals and families, and ultimately less crime and other problems arising from poverty and inequality. As it is often said, "If you think education is expensive, try ignorance."

A 2022 study published by the Fraser Institute[1] reported that Saskatchewan is one of three provinces in Canada that reduced per-student funding for education. The province went from being the highest per-student funder in 2012–2013 to the sixth highest in 2019–2020.

Yet if there is a province in Canada in need of a strong education and training system, it would be Saskatchewan, given the rate of family and child poverty.

At the same time as Saskatchewan is a world leader when it comes to potash reserves—not to mention being Canada's leading supplier of conventional oil and Canada's sole producer of uranium—it also leads in the area of child poverty. About 26 percent of Saskatchewan children live in poverty, compared to a national average of about 18 percent. Saskatchewan has the distinction, along with Manitoba, of being one of only two provinces in Canada not to have made any progress on tackling child poverty over the last decade or so.[2]

During years of economic growth, as per-student education funding declined, no progress was made in Saskatchewan to lift people out of poverty, either through the tax system by increasing transfers to low-income people or otherwise. A 2021 University of Regina study reported that during good economic times in Saskatchewan, "little if any of the economic benefits reached the poorest in the province."[3] More than a quarter of Saskatchewan children live in poverty.[4] This is the opposite of what should occur in a time of economic growth and higher profits—not unlike the relationship between higher potash profits and public share, which would also be expected to increase. It is a classic example of the rich getting richer while the poor get poorer. In fact, the depth of poverty was greater in the prairie provinces than in other Canadian provinces. In Saskatchewan, in 2019, the amount needed to boost one-half of families living in poverty above the poverty line was at least $13,482 to $16,902 per year.[5]

As profits have grown for potash producers, benefit payments to the poorest people in the province have remained the same, demonstrating year after year that the benefit amounts are not enough.[6] "The future does not bode well for low-income residents of the province—it seems likely, that when data about the province's poverty rate for 2020 becomes available, there will be a significant increase in poverty."[7] The report concludes the province is setting up a generation for failure. Inequality will become more pronounced when it should be lessened. The authors attribute this state of affairs to "indifference toward the plight of children living below the poverty line."[8]

A 2022 national study reported that among the provinces, Saskatchewan had the second highest rate of child poverty in Canada, at 19.7 percent, compared to a national average of 13.5 percent.[9]

Because social assistance benefits are inadequate to cover expenses,[10] people at the lower end of the income scale "have difficulty feeding and housing themselves and do not have the resources that would allow their protection against the negative long-term effects that poverty and discrimination have on social, mental, and physical health and well-being."[11]

In 2017, the Saskatchewan government began to phase out a rental supplement to social assistance recipients. And in 2019, social assistance to cover the recipients' cost of utilities was discontinued. Formerly, the government paid social assistance recipients' rent directly to their landlords. This practice was also discontinued. This has resulted in non-payment of rent as many social assistance families clamour to meet their expenses, and also a high rate of eviction. Thirty percent of social assistance recipients did not pay any rent at all in September and October 2021. The CEO of the Saskatchewan Landlord Association, Cameron Choquette, said: "I think the general public can look to [the] streets of Saskatoon and Regina and Prince Albert to see that evictions have increased and homelessness has increased."[12] He went on to say that, upon eviction, social assistance recipients need to come up with a security deposit for another tenancy, and the fact that this was only available to them once every two years as part of their social assistance program represented a "systemic barrier to success."[13]

Doreen Lloyd, a community outreach worker in Regina with ten years of experience, said that she "has never personally seen Regina's homelessness situation as bad as it is today."[14] She said certain policy changes had meant "homelessness has increased dramatically in the city....This is the worst I have ever seen it."[15] Lloyd cited people living in tents in the city as a result of cutbacks in social assistance.

> "It is a nightmare for a lot of our folks," said Lloyd. The SAP program directly paid rent to landlords and utilities...guaranteeing that rent was paid and shelter was provided. "They're allowed $285 for a basic allowance, which consists of their food, their transportation, and their clothing and utilities," said Lloyd....The program allots $575 for shelter in Regina and Saskatoon. "Good luck finding something in the city for $575," said Lloyd.[16]

The same article stated: "According to the Canadian Mortgage and Housing Corporation (CMHC)'s 2021 rental market report, the average cost of a rental in Regina is $1,061, while a bachelor suite specifically was $757 on average."[17] Choquette said the goal of having people manage their own funds was commendable, "but it is much harder, if not nigh-on impossible to do that if a person does not have their basic needs met."[18] He stated housing stability is necessary "so they can tackle other issues in life, whether it be mental health, addiction, domestic violence, or any number of other issues."[19]

Prior to the impact of these cutbacks in social assistance, the Saskatchewan Human Rights Commission issued a report in 2018, which stated there was a need to narrow the gap between rental allowance and the amount of actual rent, and a rental supplement was needed.[20]

Changes to social assistance in 2021 led to "a huge growth in homelessness," according to the Regina Anti-Poverty Ministry's Peter Gilmer, because "people no longer get the actual cost of their utilities covered...an individual is provided $600 to cover their rent or other housing costs and all of their utilities, and that's virtually impossible."[21] Gilmer also pointed out the Saskatchewan Assured Income for Disability program had not seen its benefits increased since 2015.[22]

Miguel Sanchez, the author of the Campaign 2000 report on child poverty in Saskatchewan, has stated that despite raising the issue of child poverty year after year, he saw "the continuity of the same socio-political, economic model that seems to privilege private interest over public interest and over people."[23]

Sanchez's analysis that there is an "economic model that seems to privilege private interest over public interest" states in a nutshell the practice of government when it comes to taxing wealthy potash companies and when it comes to obtaining a fair price for the public's potash resource.

It is difficult to disagree that private interests are in a privileged position over the public interest. Shareholders who live outside the province receive favourable treatment while the vulnerable within the province receive less as time goes on. It is inexplicable that the companies and shareholders in a situation of huge profit would be favoured over Saskatchewan people.

The cost of ending poverty in Saskatchewan was estimated to have been $547 million in 2017.[24] This is the amount the authors of the report reaching that conclusion said was needed to close the gap for families living in poverty to reach the official poverty line in 2017. This is fairly consistent with an estimate of the amount required to end poverty in Canada by bringing everyone up to the poverty line. The estimate of the federal government was $19.4 billion in 2016, which would, on a per capita basis, amount to a similar sum for Saskatchewan.[25] The 2016 Census put Canada's population at 35,151,728 in 2016, and Saskatchewan at 1,098,352.[26] Therefore, the per capita cost of closing the gap in 2016 would have been $551.89 per person in Canada and roughly $606 million for Saskatchewan. That is not far off from the University of Regina report's estimate of $547 million per year.

Jeffrey Sachs, a world-renowned economist, wrote in 2006 that poverty in the world could be eliminated at a cost of $235 billion per year for twenty years, less than one percent of the combined income of the richest countries in the world.[27]

There are convincing arguments that poverty costs Canada and Saskatchewan many billions of dollars per year. Canada's National Council of Welfare declared in 2022 that health and justice system expenditures and loss of productive capacity resulting from poverty and underdevelopment of human potential occurred at a great cost. The Council argued that spending in various areas such as early childhood development and support for families would save many dollars for every dollar spent because of decreased costs dealing with the effects of poverty on health, educational outcomes, and so on.

Without going into the valid arguments that eradicating poverty would probably save money in the long run by reducing costs in other areas and improving economic output, there is no reason for poverty to exist in Saskatchewan. It can actually be eradicated, given the natural resource wealth the province has. What it takes is the political will to do so.

In a 2019 paper, Dr. Charles Plante estimated that poverty costs Saskatchewan $3.8 billion each year, broken down as follows:

- $420 million in higher health care costs
- $50 to $120 million in additional criminal justice system spending
- $2.6 billion in lost contributions to GDP and taxes
- $720 million in higher social assistance spending

He pointed out that ending poverty is "the right thing to do" and "also the smart thing to do."[28]

Along with the province's record in child poverty, Saskatchewan continues to have the highest rate of incarceration in Canada. In 2018–2019, the province jailed 215 per 100,000 people compared to the national rate of 127 per 100,000 people. And Saskatchewan's youth incarceration rate was 14 per 10,000 youth compared to the national rate of 4 per 10,000 youth.[29]

In tandem with high child and family poverty and high incarceration rates are Saskatchewan's low educational attainment levels. The Conference Board of Canada gives Saskatchewan, Manitoba, New Brunswick, and Newfoundland and Labrador all "D"s on education and skills. It notes that Saskatchewan and Manitoba have managed to lag behind other provinces while enjoying newfound resource activity and higher taxable resource development.[30]

Social assistance rates in Saskatchewan are below Canada's official poverty line, leaving most recipients "living in deep poverty in 2020."[31] The 2023–2024 Saskatchewan budget, "Growth That Works for Everyone," provided people receiving social assistance with an increase of $1 per day during a time of high inflation.

The various examples of budget choices set out above resulted from an expressed shortage of revenue to government. The unmet needs of Saskatchewan people are relevant when considering questions about resource ownership: whether purely private ownership best serves the public interest, what a reasonable rate of profit should be, and how a royalty and taxation system should operate.

My purpose in relaying this gloomy information is not to depress people or trash Saskatchewan, my home province, where I live and a place I love. It is to place questions of taxation in context so that in considering matters of public policy there is an appreciation that choices in one area impact other areas profoundly. As well, an appreciation of some social realities in the province assists in answering the question whether Saskatchewan needs more resources to deal with important objectives. To that, surely the answer must be a resounding "Yes!"

The context is important in assessing whether obtaining a greater share of the profits for the public produced from their resources is a significant issue or would change anything. The reality is that, for many, it could change everything.

The most vulnerable in society generally do not have voices who speak for them consistently and loudly. Lip service is paid to our belief in equality of opportunity and determination to end child poverty. Actions do not always seem to be consistent with statements of belief and intention. People generally are in favour of fighting poverty and inequality. Yet the reality is sometimes ignored. Doing things required to improve the lot of people in lower socio-economic brackets doesn't just benefit them. It benefits everyone through healthier societies with less incarceration and other ills that accompany poverty. It makes everyone feel better and more secure about their society.

Saskatchewan has been on the forefront of public policy in the past. It is where hospitalization without billing the patient was started in 1948, a program taken nationally by Prime Minister John Diefenbaker, who was from Saskatchewan, a decade later. It is where medicare, which ensures equal access to medical services regardless of financial means, was implemented in 1962, thanks to the leadership of Tommy Douglas, Woodrow Lloyd, and their colleagues in government. A national program gradually emerged thanks to the work of former Supreme Court Justice Emmett Hall, also from Saskatchewan, who was appointed by Prime Minister Diefenbaker to head a commission to recommend how medical services should be provided in Canada. That commission recommended the model in place in Saskatchewan be taken nationally. After the defeat of the Diefenbaker government, Liberal prime ministers Lester B. Pearson and Pierre Trudeau oversaw the implementation of medicare across the country, one province at a time. Here was a Liberal government implementing the recommendation of a commission set up by the previous Progressive Conservative government to adopt a program developed by the Saskatchewan NDP government. This example serves to illustrate the important role that Saskatchewan has historically played in developing positive social policy in Canada. It is also an example of representatives of three political parties looking beyond ideology on the role of the market or the private sector and objectively seeking solutions that best meet the overall public interest.

Children need food and clothing. They need school supplies. Hundreds of dollars to support them today to enhance their well-being and prospects may prevent society from spending $100,000 per year twenty years from now to put them in jail because we did not equip them to succeed. Many a credible study has demonstrated that better social support reduces poverty, crime, addiction, and other social problems.

That social spending has been suppressed when potash producers' profits have skyrocketed is very difficult to understand. Political leaders are not needed to speak for the rich and powerful. They can speak for themselves or hire people to speak for them. It is the government's job to seek the public interest. Political leaders should be concerned about the most vulnerable in society. They cannot fix everything, but they can improve some things.

So that there is no misunderstanding, as people I have worked with know, I am not a bleeding-heart liberal. I believe people need to work hard to take advantage of the opportunities before them. For people to succeed, however, we need to recognize we don't all come out of the same starting gate. We need to take steps to give all people the tools required to succeed, to enable them to put in the work they need to do to make their way. It isn't easy, and it takes time. That's no reason not to start. It's a reason to get going.

CONCLUSION

Fifty years ago, we recognized that having the world's largest reserves of potash was a great legacy for Saskatchewan. There was a belief that, as other countries had seen, the resource could be transformative for society. Public policy was conceived that demanded expansion of the industry to supplant less efficient operations in the United States, and demanded maximum benefit be achieved for the people of the province. The government of the day believed that ensuring Saskatchewan people had a say in the manner of development would help meet these objectives. Leaders with this vision established that a small province of one million people could overcome obstacles industry put in place and that, at the end of the day, the government of Saskatchewan, on behalf of the people of the province, must have the final word when it comes to developing the province's resources.

For a time, the three-fold policy of expansion, public benefit, and Saskatchewan participation in market decisions was achieved. Unlike the ultimately popular medicare program established by Saskatchewan residents in the decade prior to the establishment of the Potash Corporation of Saskatchewan, the government failed to convince enough people in Saskatchewan of the wisdom of its approach. The vision and its achievement were abandoned without significant public outcry after fourteen years of successful operation.

Privatization was made easier by difficult times in the world potash market and a public asset was sold off at the bottom of the market. Gradually, the industry built up and returned to good profits. The creation of PCS as a Crown corporation established the largest potash company in the world, thereby making Saskatchewan, for the first time, not simply a location for branch plants, but a place where decisions were made and profits could be kept.

The 1970s acquisition of five operating mines at fair market value to create PCS as a Crown corporation was a precursor to further consolidation in the industry, which over the course of forty years culminated, for a time, in two potash giants, PCS and Mosaic, which owned and operated nine of the original potash mines operating in Saskatchewan. Agrium operated the tenth at Vanscoy. K+S developed the Bethune mine between 2011 and 2017. Now, BHP will also enter potash mining in Saskatchewan.

As the private corporate model took hold in the privatized PCS, the Saskatchewan-focused decision-making aspects of the original plan and the limits on ownership outside the province gradually, and probably inevitably, gave way to corporate decision-making without Saskatchewan as the key focus. World demand increased with world population, a growing world middle class, and the education of farmers throughout the world about the benefits of fertilization. Profits soared, and the world noticed. BHP made a bid for PCS, which was disallowed. The eventual surrender of PCS into the merged Nutrien occurred with PCS shareholders receiving less than 40 percent of the amount BHP had offered PCS shareholders. While BHP's goal of acquiring PCS mines in Saskatchewan was anathema to PCS and the governments of Saskatchewan and Canada, the merger of PCS into a vertically integrated fertilizer retailer with priorities far beyond profitability of its potash assets went virtually unnoticed, as if there was no Saskatchewan interest to be considered.

At the same time, the volume and value of potash sold, and profits earned, soared steadily to hitherto unknown heights. Just as the goals of Saskatchewan direction and ownership had been abandoned, knowledgeable observers from various perspectives (left, right, and centre) pointed out that the goal of maximizing financial return to the people of Saskatchewan appeared to be gone as well. If PCS's profits, which belonged to the public when it was a Crown corporation, were to be given up as they were in 1989, the people of the province had the right to expect they would receive a good return for a valuable asset. That has not occurred for the last fifteen years.

Government, inexplicably, rejected even a review of the situation.

In the Saudi Arabia of potash, shortages in the public treasury resulted in government taking away from the most vulnerable, raising sales tax, and favouring the potash industry over other sectors of the economy.

Little consideration appears to have been given to the most logical source of public funding. A method to address shortfalls in public spending and some serious social issues in Saskatchewan, through the adoption of a different model of potash royalty and taxation such as economic rents, is readily available but consciously avoided.

Past policy-makers provided a vision of how the potash resource could be used as a powerful asset to improve the well-being of Saskatchewan people and were aware of the consequences of their actions in both the short-term and long-term interests of Saskatchewan. Can it be said that vision and foresight have continued to be evident in managing Saskatchewan's potash legacy?

Saskatchewan has become a spectator of the potash/fertilizer retailing business and a passive recipient of the impact of its decisions, simply waiting for the next move of the corporate giants, who are believed to be more capable of making decisions in an industry that is effectively a monopoly in the free world and trusted to make decisions in Saskatchewan's interests. The potash companies cannot be blamed for pursuing what is in the best interests of the companies and their shareholders. That's their job. Maximizing public interest is the job of government.

The potash industry has secured strong public support through investment, employment, and charitable contributions and sponsorships. These factors, and perhaps a lack of awareness of financial outcomes and profit levels, have brought about a complacency not characteristic of the 1960s and 1970s.

If Saskatchewan has decided a purely private model of potash mining is to remain, it is still open to the province to ensure it obtains a reasonable economic rent for its potash. Tax tools can be used to encourage investment and the maintenance of mining and indirect spinoff jobs in Saskatchewan, and head office jobs as well. The province can still insist it not be regarded as an irrelevant backwater no one would want to live in and let it be known the people of the province are the owners of the resource. The province can still engage in dialogue with industry and insist upon being consulted about the direction of the industry. It can make it clear it does not take kindly to foreign ownership so unaware of the realities of Canadian affairs that a conversation with a former federal minister can represent a relevant conversation about potash with the people of Saskatchewan. The province should be respectful in its dealings with the private sector and should expect respectful treatment from the private sector. Respectful treatment of the private sector does not include kowtowing to private capital or believing that it is always the best vehicle to maximize profit, given the track record of maximizing shareholder value, which is a matter of public record.

Many people believe the government doesn't know how to run a business, that PCS was a failed and costly venture as a Crown corporation, and that its creation frightened investment away from Saskatchewan. They believe it was sold to private parties more able to diversify and grow the company, thereby generating economic activity that circulates throughout Saskatchewan. This narrative has been promoted by the defenders of the private model.

Looking at the facts objectively, including the financial performance of PCS as a Crown corporation, the potash industry's recovery in the 1990s, the fact that no potash owner other than the Saskatchewan government sold their mines off in 1989 at the bottom of the market, and, finally, the industry's financial returns, it is difficult to accept that narrative.

An alternative narrative is as follows: PCS's privatization caused a loss of tens of billions of dollars to Saskatchewan. The province sold infrastructure and assets when no one else did, in an industry that cannot go anywhere and in which it is not difficult to make a lot of money. After preventing BHP from making an offer to PCS shareholders, the Saskatchewan government stood idly by as PCS was integrated into a multinational fertilizer conglomerate that aims to have an economical source of potash for its fertilizer retail operations. Having opted for full private ownership, the province still could have obtained maximum value from the sale of its potash but has chosen not to do so. For fifteen years, voices on the right and left of the political spectrum, as well as people in the centre, have offered expert analysis to the government, identifying a serious problem and offering a solution. The Saskatchewan government, rather than following the advice of independent experts, has instead relied upon the advice of experts from the industry itself. When confronted by poverty, a crisis in health care, an education system crying out for more resources to prepare Saskatchewan children for a successful life, and a high rate of poverty, incarceration, and homelessness, the wealthiest corporations operating in the province are under-taxed while the government cuts back on the poorest of the poor.

The province can set aside the notion that what is good for big business is good for Saskatchewan, and bargain hard on behalf of the people of the province. It is apparent that has not been occurring for some time.

If, contrary to this book's thesis, the industry and the Saskatchewan government assert that public policy is as it should be, and status quo taxes and royalties are the best we can do for Saskatchewan, then neither the government nor the potash companies should be averse to an objective and transparent public inquiry into the costs and profits of the potash industry. The potash industry's significance to Saskatchewan, and to some extent Canada, demands that the public be assured the balance of reward between the industry and the people of the province is appropriate. It is perhaps the most important question the province faces because the resolution of the question may enable the province to deal with some serious social issues, which could be addressed. It is not an exaggeration to say that the outcome of the issue will determine what kind of province Saskatchewan will be: a land characterized by progress and equal opportunity, or an economically stratified community containing large pockets of prosperity and large pockets of despair.

Saudi Arabia and Norway figured out decades ago how to maximize return for their countries. Saskatchewan should not squander the world-class legacy it has through devotion to ideology, or some misguided notion we cannot be hard-nosed bargainers with large foreign companies.

Any advocate will have a view that what they are advocating for is fair. Fairness is a two-way street. What is fair to one may be unfair to another. Everything requires an appropriate balance. When it comes to the question of whether revenue to government for the extraction of non-renewable resources is fair, it involves considering whether the public is receiving a fair price for its resource, and whether the potash mining company is receiving a fair return on its investment.

Government's role is to relentlessly pursue the public interest, not private interests, corporate interests, ideological interests, or other interests. Public interest demands there be an environmentally sustainable, profitable, and effective potash industry in Saskatchewan, whether private, public, or a combination thereof. Saskatchewan has enough potash reserves to supply the world for a thousand years. It is not going to run out of it anytime soon, and it should have a strong industry bringing jobs, economic spinoffs, and public benefit through contributions to the public treasury.

It is abundantly clear that the division of profits from potash mining is grossly unbalanced. The province is shortchanging its own treasury and its people. A significant change is urgently needed and long overdue.

The evolution of the pioneering companies that built potash mines in Saskatchewan in the 1960s provides a very interesting tale. In some ways, Saskatchewan has gone back to where it started. It receives some of the revenue from foreign interests mining its potash but has no ongoing influence or control over the world market or ability to influence job numbers, layoffs, job security, or aspects of local economic spinoff. The lack of these levers was part of the motivation of Saskatchewan politicians who sought to maximize public interest from the potash resource.

Still, notwithstanding everything, unless the government decides to sell off the potash resource itself, the province will continue to control royalty and taxation rates. Therefore, an appreciation of provincial interests is in the industry's interests. Even fifty years later, corporate executives will remember that the leaders of a small province can only be pushed so far without pushing back. Leaders of large corporations in twenty-first century North America undoubtedly have a better understanding of that than may have been the case in the 1960s and 1970s.

Saskatchewan's birthright is a resource so sufficiently vast, rich, and in demand that it could enable the province to build a model society. The province can have quality education, health care, and programming for the benefit of all its citizens. It can end poverty and homelessness. It can leave more earnings in the pockets of working people and the coffers of industries other than potash. It can do these things if it decides to.

At the end of the day, both government leaders and industry leaders should understand the question of how the balance of fairness between the industry and public is achieved involves not just consideration of whether farmers in the United States enjoy the benefit of low-cost fertilizer components or whether shareholder value has been maximized. It also involves considering how excess profits should be shared, if the tax burden on average citizens could be lessened, and if a large cohort of disadvantaged youth, along with all Saskatchewan citizens, enjoy the benefit of everything their society can do to achieve greater equal opportunity and a better quality of life through responsible and wise stewardship of the resources Saskatchewan has been blessed with.

ACKNOWLEDGEMENTS

Several people with experience and expert knowledge in potash and resource taxation provided insightful comments after generously taking the time to review parts of this book primarily dealing with financial matters and analysis at various drafting stages. The outcome was greatly improved because of their expert advice. I am indebted to Jack Mintz, Erin Weir, Ron Styles, Jim Marshall, and Greg Marchildon for comments and suggestions, and to Jim Stanford for reviewing the manuscript. My wife, Pauline Melis, provided invaluable assistance formatting various drafts of the manuscript and offered helpful suggestions to ensure clarity in a number of cases. As well, she patiently allowed me to spend many hours over a long period of time researching and writing. Anonymous reviewers on behalf of the University of Regina Press provided insightful comments and valid suggestions for correction, clarification, and elaboration of many points, all of which greatly improved the final manuscript. I am very grateful to the able staff and associates of the University of Regina Press, whose professional advice and efforts greatly improved the book, or made its production possible, including Shannon Parr, Adrineh Der-Boghossian, David McLennan, Jellyn Ayudan, Duncan Campbell, Judy Dunlop, Melissa Shirley, and Curran Faris.

VALUE OF POTASH SALES AND PAYMENTS TO PUBLIC TREASURY, 1962–2022[1]

Year	Value of Sales (Can$000)	Public Revenue (Can$ million)	Percent Revenue to Sales (%)
1962	3,000	n/a	—
1963	22,500	n/a	—
1964	31,162	n/a	—
1965	55,971	1.10	1.96
1966	62,665	1.90	3.03
1967	67,395	2.20	3.26
1968	65,121	2.10	3.22
1969	69,383	2.90	4.17
1970	108,695	2.70	2.48
1971	145,966	2.80	1.91
1972	146,014	5.60	3.83
1973	195,025	8.30	4.25
1974	311,621	34.60	11.10
1975	348,494	80.70	23.15
1976	358,399	96.10	26.81

Year	Value of Sales (Can$000)	Public Revenue (Can$ million)	Percent Revenue to Sales (%)
1977	389,694	109.80	28.17
1978	492,473	125.30	25.44
1979	730,636	152.10	20.81
1980	1,007,418	228.30	22.66
1981	989,940	264.70	26.90
1982	632,480	80.60	12.74
1983	674,367	41.20	6.10
1984	802,342	64.80	8.07
1985	599,199	45.30	7.56
1986	542,728	34.00	6.26
1987	649,162	36.50	5.62
1988	932,496	83.40	8.94
1989	848,313	69.00	8.13
1990	784,258	30.90	3.94
1991	765,000	48.50	6.33
1992	812,000	53.80	6.62
1993	800,000	84.40	10.55
1994	1,109,000	111.10	10.00
1995	1,217,000	136.90	11.25
1996	1,116,000	149.00	13.35
1997	1,505,000	160.40	10.66
1998	1,624,000	274.30	16.90
1999	1,682,000	228.45	13.58
2000	1,744,000	216.10	12.39
2001	1,622,000	238.05	14.68
2002	1,718,000	236.86	13.79
2003	1,632,000	188.93	11.58
2004	2,168,000	383.49	17.69
2005	2,697,000	373.94	13.90

Year	Value of Sales (Can$000)	Public Revenue (Can$ million)	Percent Revenue to Sales (%)
2006	2,210,000	228.00	10.32
2007	3,056,000	524.47	17.16
2008	7,386,000	1,585.62	21.46
2009	3,067,000	(-91.89)	0
2010	5,366,000	430.04	8.01
2011	6,714,000	643.97	9.60
2012	5,972,000	543.65	9.10
2013	5,609,000	514.33	9.17
2014	5,699,900	517.25	9.10
2015	6,096,500	736.07	12.10
2016	4,181,500	366.43	8.80
2017	4,763,300	452.28	9.40
2018	5,712,900	716.0	12.53
2019	6,287,000	733.03	11.66
2020	5,467,000	625.62	11.44
2021	7,556,000	1,453.5	19.24
2022	17,983,000	2,894.19	16.10

POTASH PRODUCTION VOLUME AND AVERAGE PRICE, 1997–2022[2]

Year	Volume of Potash Production (000s Tonnes)	Average Price (Can$)
1997	8,297	172.61
1998	8,035	202.18
1999	7,975	204.78
2000	8,601.9	197.57
2001	7,785	205.93
2002	8,154.3	210.82
2003	8,638.4	185.60
2004	9,638.1	216.82
2005	10,133.2	282.66
2006	7,919.2	296.16
2007	10,661.4	286.71
2008	9,390.4	746.54
2009	4,250.6	809.03
2010	9,108.5	569.74
2011	10,377.9	666.95
2012	8,825.5	583.53
2013	9,737.5	486.12

Year	Volume of Potash Production (000s Tonnes)	Average Price (Can$)
2014	10,273.5	575.44
2015	11,124.7	373.19
2016	10,966.1	383.96
2017	12,407.4	440.97
2018	13,143.2	457
2019	12,559.1	490
2020	13,722,4	387.31
2021	14,241.8	567.80
2022	14,354.9	1,334.80

NOTES

I. THE IMPORTANCE OF POTASH

1   Peterson, "Deputy PM Visits."

2   Peterson, "Deputy PM Visits."

3   Dollar figures throughout this book are in Canadian dollars except where otherwise indicated.

4   Friedman, "BHP Accelerates Work."

5   Friedman, "BHP Accelerates Work."

6   MacPherson, "The 100-Day War."

7   This point is developed and source material for it is referenced in chapters 6 and 7.

8   Elferink and Schierhorn, "Global Demand."

9   Silva, "Feeding the World."

10   Potash Corporation of Saskatchewan 2015 annual report, 2–3.

11   Natural Resources Canada, *Potash Facts*.

12   Natural Resources Canada, *Potash Facts*.

13   Price increases and projected high prices in the years ahead are discussed and source-referenced in chapter 8.

14   Natural Resources Canada, *Potash Facts*.

15   The Mosaic Company, timetodigdeeper.com.

16   Saskatchewan's Dashboard on Business and Economy.

17   Natural Resources Canada, *Gold Facts*.

18   The Canadian Pacific Railway (CPR) was granted mineral rights in Western Canada to assist the development of the transcontinental railway in the 1880s. Hudson's Bay Company was similarly given mineral rights in Western Canada in return for relinquishing its land rights to the federal government after Confederation in 1867.

19   Government of Saskatchewan, Economic Overview 2020, 4.

20   Saskatchewan's Dashboard on Business and Economy.

21   Government of Saskatchewan, 2023–24 budget documents.

22 Government of Saskatchewan, Economic Overview 2020, 2.

23 Government of Saskatchewan, Economic Overview 2020, 2.

24 2019 OPEC *Annual Statistical Bulletin*.

25 2019 OPEC *Annual Statistical Bulletin*.

26 Fattouh, *Saudi Oil Policy*.

27 Norwegian Petroleum Directorate, Norwegian Ministry of Petroleum and Energy.

28 Norwegian Petroleum Directorate, Norwegian Ministry of Petroleum and Energy.

29 Norwegian Petroleum Directorate, Norwegian Ministry of Petroleum and Energy.

30 Hsieh, "What Norway Did with Its Oil."

2. BRANCH PLANT POTASH MINE DEVELOPMENT

1 All preceding information of a factual nature in this chapter is taken from Fuzesy, *Geological Report* 181.

2 Blakeney, *An Honourable Calling*, 141.

3. PUBLIC OWNERSHIP THROUGH THE POTASH CORPORATION OF SASKATCHEWAN

1 Rediger, *The Crowns*, 105.

2 Blakeney, *An Honourable Calling*, 139–140.

3 Blakeney, *An Honourable Calling*, 148.

4 Debates and Proceedings of the Legislative Assembly of Saskatchewan, 420.

5 Rediger, *The Crowns*, 106.

6 Burton, Potash.

7 Rediger, *The Crowns*, 107.

8 Blakeney, *An Honourable Calling*, 145–50.

9 Blakeney, *An Honourable Calling*, 150.

10 Blakeney, *An Honourable Calling*, 150.

11 Blakeney, *An Honourable Calling*, 150.

12 Blakeney, *An Honourable Calling*, 150–151.

13 Blakeney, *An Honourable Calling*, 151.

14 Rediger, *The Crowns*, 107. David Dombowsky, former deputy minister of finance, was named board chair of PCS, and several engineers and managers from some of the potash companies were recruited to the initial management structure. See also Gruending, *Promises to Keep*, 142–143. Millionaire entrepreneur and nationalist Maurice Strong and retired Ottawa senior public servant Douglas Fullerton were advisors to Blakeney. Fullerton served on the early PCS board.

15 *Journals of the Legislative Assembly*, 6.

16 *Journals of the Legislative Assembly*, 6.

17 *Journals of the Legislative Assembly*, 8.

18 *Journals of the Legislative Assembly*, 8.

19 *Journals of the Legislative Assembly*, 8.

20 *Journals of the Legislative Assembly*, 8–9.

21 *Journals of the Legislative Assembly*, 7.

22 *Journals of the Legislative Assembly*, 8.

23 Debates and Proceedings of the Legislative Assembly of Saskatchewan, 416.

24 Debates and Proceedings of the Legislative Assembly of Saskatchewan, 417.

25 Debates and Proceedings of the Legislative Assembly of Saskatchewan, 417.

26 Rediger, *The Crowns*, 107.

27 Rediger, *The Crowns*, 109.

28 Rediger, *The Crowns*, 109.

29 Rediger, *The Crowns*, 109.

30 Olewiler, *The Potash Corporation of Saskatchewan*, 39–40.

31 Rediger, *The Crowns*, 109.

32 Burton, *Potash*, 112.

33 Burton, *Potash*, 113.

34 Rediger, *The Crowns*, 109.

35 Olewiler, *The Potash Corporation*; Blakeney, *An Honourable Calling*.

36 Blakeney, *An Honourable Calling*, 153.

37 Blakeney, *An Honourable Calling*, 153–154.

38 Blakeney, *An Honourable Calling*, 154.

39 Moore and Vining, *The Privatization of Potash Corporation of Saskatchewan*.

40 Romanow, *Building on Values*.

41 Christopher, "Single Payer Healthcare"; Kurtzman, *Single-Payer Systems Likely to Save Money in US*.

42 Olewiler, *The Potash Corporation of Saskatchewan*, 17.

43 Olewiler, *The Potash Corporation of Saskatchewan*, 39.

44 Moore and Vining, *The Privatization of Potash Corporation of Saskatchewan*, 12.

45 Moore and Vining, *The Privatization of Potash Corporation of Saskatchewan*, 12.

46 Moore and Vining, *The Privatization of Potash Corporation of Saskatchewan*, 12.

47 Moore and Vining, *The Privatization of Potash Corporation of Saskatchewan*, 12.

48 Moore and Vining, *The Privatization of Potash Corporation of Saskatchewan*, 12.

49 Olewiler, *The Potash Corporation of Saskatchewan*, 93.

50 Olewiler, *The Potash Corporation of Saskatchewan*, 93.

51 Burton, *Potash*, 109.

52 Burton, *Potash*, 98.

53 Burton, *Potash*, 102.

54 Burton, *Potash*, 98.

55 Burton, *Potash*, 109–110.

56 Burton, *Potash*, 110.

57 Burton, *Potash*, 110.

58 Burton, *Potash*, 112–113.

59 Burton, *Potash*, 118.

60 Olewiler, *The Potash Corporation of Saskatchewan*, 37–38.

61 Olewiler, *The Potash Corporation of Saskatchewan*, 39–41.

62 Burton, *Potash*, 120–121.

63 Burton, *Potash*, 118.

64 Burton, *Potash*, 122–124.

65 Burton, *Potash*, 125.

66 Burton, *Potash*, 130.

4. PRIVATIZATION OF THE POTASH CORPORATION OF SASKATCHEWAN

1 Moore and Vining, *The Privatization of Potash Corporation of Saskatchewan*, 12.

2 Olewiler, *The Potash Corporation of Saskatchewan*, 92.

3 Charlton et al., *The Privatization of the Potash Corporation of Saskatchewan*, 3, as cited in Warnock, *Exploiting Saskatchewan's Potash*, 17.

4 Burton, *Potash*, 141.

5 Burton, *Potash*; Blakeney, *An Honourable Calling*; Rediger, *The Crowns*; Olewiler, *The Potash Corporation of Saskatchewan*; Charlton et al., *The Privatization of the Potash Corporation of Saskatchewan*. Blakeney, Burton, and Charlton were all associated with the NDP government of Saskatchewan in the 1970s. They are, however, respected and credible writers and entitled to present facts that are open to challenge. Their writings have not been challenged. Even Moore and Vining, *The Privatization of Potash Corporation of Saskatchewan*, were unable to convincingly state PCS was not successful financially and doubted that privatization would be a financial benefit to the Saskatchewan people.

6 Burton, *Potash*, 108–109 and 114.

7 PCS *Annual Report*, 1997.

8 Burton, *Potash*, 140.

9 Burton, *Potash*, 140–141.

10 Weir, "Maximize Public Gain from Potash."

11 Weir, "Privatizing Potash Was a Costly Mistake."

12 Pitts, "PotashCorp.'s Bill Doyle Dims Hope for New Mines."

13 McNish et al., "Potash: The Deal That Didn't Have to Die."

14 Ladurantaye, "Bill Doyle's Modest Return."

15 Olewiler, *The Potash Corporation of Saskatchewan*, 85.

5. POTASH MINES CAN'T BE MOVED TO CHICAGO

1 Silcoff, "It Takes Chutzpah."

2 Government of Saskatchewan, "Balanced Budget Keeping Saskatchewan Strong."

3 Chen and Mintz, "Fixing Saskatchewan's Potash Royalty Mess" and "Potash Taxation."

4   Information compiled from Agrium, PCS, and Mosaic annual reports
    for 2005 and 2021, and Government of Saskatchewan news release
    "Saskatchewan Potash Producers Ramp Up Production."

5   Government of Saskatchewan, "Potash Sector Sets New Records."

6   See appendix B for average annual prices.

7   Government of Saskatchewan, "Potash Sector Sets New Records."

8   All numbers are compiled from Saskatchewan Finance, Saskatchewan
    Bureau of Statistics, Saskatchewan Provincial Economic Account, 2021
    edition.

6. INTEGRATION OF THE POTASH CORPORATION
OF SASKATCHEWAN INTO NUTRIEN

1   IndexMundi, Potassium Chloride Monthly Price.

2   "Potash Corp Urges Rejection."

3   McCullough, "What Investors Still Don't Understand About Nutrien."

4   Potash Corporation of Saskatchewan, "PotashCorp's 'Pledge to
    Saskatchewan.'"

5   Government of Saskatchewan, "Premier Welcomes 'Pledge to
    Saskatchewan.'"

6   MacPherson, "Premier Wall Says He Expects Head-Office Pledge."

7   MacPherson, "Premier Wall Says He Expects Head-Office Pledge."

8   MacPherson, "Premier Wall Says He Expects Head-Office Pledge."

9   MacPherson, "Premier Wall Says He Expects Head-Office Pledge."

10 MacPherson, "Wall Pledges to Look at 'Every Option.'"

11 MacPherson, "Wall Pledges to Look at 'Every Option.'"

12 MacPherson, "Wall Pledges to Look at 'Every Option.'"

13 MacPherson, "Wall Pledges to Look at 'Every Option.'"

14 Giles, "Wall Blasts PotashCorp."

15 Nutrien, *2019 Annual Report*, 29.

16 McCullough, "What Investors Still Don't Understand."

17 McCullough, "What Investors Still Don't Understand."

18 McCullough, "What Investors Still Don't Understand."

19 McCullough, "What Investors Still Don't Understand."

20 McCullough, "What Investors Still Don't Understand."

21 McCullough, "What Investors Still Don't Understand."

22 Cited in McCullough, "What Investors Still Don't Understand."

23 Nutrien, *Annual Report 2018*, 2.

24 Nutrien, *Annual Report 2018*, 1.

25 Nutrien, *Annual Report 2022*, 7.

26 Nutrien, *Providing Solutions for a Growing World*, 6.

27 Nutrien, *Annual Report 2019*, 19.

28 Nutrien, *Annual Report 2022*, 7.

7. CONSEQUENCES OF CHOICES MADE IN 1989, 2010, AND 2018

1   Nutrien, *Annual Report 2019*, 29.
2   Nutrien, *Annual Report 2019*, 12.

8. THE PROFITS OF POTASH

1   Burton, *Potash*, 194.
2   Burton, *Potash*, 194.
3   Burton, *Potash*, 194–95.
4   Bank of Canada inflation calculator.
5   Saskatchewan's Dashboard on Business and Economy.
6   Compiled from annual figures set out in appendix A, which is based upon a format set out in appendix G of Burton, *Potash*, and reproduces his figures for 1962–1992 inclusive. For subsequent years, government revenue and volume of sales have been compiled from provincial budgets and statistics published by the ministry responsible for mineral resources, the name of which has changed over the years. The applicable 3 to 3.6 percent resource surcharge has been added to the figures for government revenue as appropriate. Where figures vary from estimates for the year in question due to adjustments in subsequent years, the figures from subsequent years are used. As well, the value of sales data has been sourced from the ministry's mineral sales reports. The potash companies' fiscal year ends on December 31; the Government of Saskatchewan's fiscal year ends on March 31. Therefore, the value of sales figures is based on the calendar year whereas public revenue is based on the government's fiscal year. In some cases, payments to the government are made after the calendar year. The relationship between the two sets of figures, however, is consistent throughout the entire period and therefore provides a continuous and valid method of comparison.
7   Chen and Mintz, "Potash Taxation."
8   Marshall, *Saskatchewan Potash Taxes and Royalties*, 10.
9   Mintz, "The Potash Royalty Mess."
10 Chen and Mintz, "Fixing Saskatchewan's Potash Royalty Mess."
11 Chen and Mintz, "Potash Taxation."
12 In determining revenue and gross profit, the minor amounts of potash produced by the companies outside of Saskatchewan are considered.
13 The yearly gross margin for potash, and company-wide, for PCS is taken from its annual reports 1995–2017.
14 Weir, "Privatizing Potash Was a Costly Mistake."
15 All data taken from PCS annual reports for the years in question or as updated in subsequent annual reports where applicable. Sales and gross profit figures for the years 1995–2015 inclusive are reduced to 92 percent of reported figures to account for potash production from New Brunswick PCS Inc. mines during that period.

16   All data taken from Agrium annual reports for the years in question or as revised in subsequent annual reports where applicable.

17   All data taken from Nutrien annual reports for the years in question.

18   All data taken from Mosaic annual reports for the years in question and, for 2021, from Mosaic's Form 10-K filing with the U.S. Securities and Exchange Commission. Sales and gross profit figures are reduced to 90 percent to account for Mosaic's possible U.S. and Brazil production, the value and grade of which was calculated as indicated by Mosaic's Form 10-K filing for 2021.

19   All data taken from IMC Global Inc Form 10-K filed 1998 and 1999, for 1995–99 years; IMC Global Inc SEC Form 10-K filed 2002 and 2003 for the years 2000–03 inclusive; and Mosaic's *Annual Report 2005*, for 2004.

20   Saskatchewan's Dashboard on Business and Economy.

21   Gross profits of K+S are not known and not included. Amounts, if any, of payments by K+S to the public treasury are not known or deducted from the public share total. Individual company payments are confidential information, and no assumptions can be made because K+S is a new mine and capital cost tax incentives would factor into the calculation of taxation.

22   Currency exchange rates taken from PCS annual reports for the years in question.

23   Where currencies are converted over multiple years, the Bank of Canada inflation calculator has been used. This calculator uses the Consumer Price Index, which is not an exact index for all purposes because it deals with a basket of consumer goods. However, the result would not be very different by using a different index and for the purpose of discussion the result would not appreciably alter the analysis. For annual conversion of U.S. dollars into Canadian dollars, as indicated in the footnote to table 7, the currency exchange rates used by PCS as indicated in its annual reports for the year in question have been used.

24   Government of Saskatchewan, "Potash Sector Sets New Records."

25   Thring, "Alberta, Oil, and the Constitution," 69.

26   Thring, "Alberta, Oil, and the Constitution," 69.

27   A full listing of annual potash production volumes and average annual prices is contained in appendix B.

28   Potash production volume figures taken from Saskatchewan Bureau of Statistics, Economic Review 2021 and Economic Review Excel Tables for the years 1998–2021 inclusive, and for 2022, from Saskatchewan's Dashboard on Business and Economy. Average potash prices for 1997–2008 inclusive, and for potash production value from 1997 are taken from Saskatchewan Ministry of Energy and Resources, Mineral Statistics Yearbook 2008, 208–210. Average potash prices for 2009–2022 inclusive are taken from Saskatchewan's Ministry of Finance annual budget documents for the years following the years in question.

29   Average percentage public share is not necessarily the average of public share to sales volume because the average percentage public share simply is

the average percent each year for the period added together and multiplied by the number of years.

30 Bank of Canada inflation calculator.

31 Saskatchewan's Dashboard on Business and Economy.

32 Nutrien, *Annual Report 2022*, 4.

33 Appendix A contains the government percentage for all years.

34 Saskatchewan budget documents, Tables of Interprovincial Taxes and Charges for 2008–2009 and 2023–2024.

35 Table 7 illustrates this was adjusted in 2009, when the industry paid no taxes or royalties once adjustments were made because the government had overstated, at least in the context of the current tax and royalty system, the amount required to be paid in 2008.

36 See table 7.

37 See appendix B.

38 PCS, *Annual Report 2007*, 2.

39 PCS, *Annual Report 2007*, 2.

40 PCS, *Annual Report 2007*, 7.

41 PCS, *Annual Report 2007*, 6.

42 The base price of 2007 is adjusted for inflation according to the Bank of Canada inflation calculator in the second column. The actual average price per year, taken from Appendix B, is in the next column. The difference between the two (i.e., the amount that could be viewed as windfall revenue) is in the third column. The tonnes produced, taken from Appendix B, appear in the third column. For the years 2018–2022 inclusive, the figures in Appendix B have been reduced to take into account production at the K+S Bethune mine, since the gross profit of K+S for those years is not known or included. Gross profit is then estimated by taking the annual potash sales of PCS, Agrium, Nutrien, and Mosaic for the years each was in production from 2008 to 2022.

43 Mintz, "Brad Wall's Good Potash Play."

44 Mintz, "Brad Wall's Good Potash Play."

45 Mintz, "Brad Wall's Good Potash Play."

46 Mills, "Saskatchewan Losing Billions in Potash Royalties."

47 Chen and Mintz, "Potash Taxation."

48 Chen and Mintz, "Potash Taxation," 8.

49 Chen and Mintz, "Fixing Saskatchewan's Potash Royalty Mess," 8.

50 Chen and Mintz, "Fixing Saskatchewan's Potash Royalty Mess," 11.

51 Chen and Mintz, "Fixing Saskatchewan's Potash Royalty Mess," 14.

52 The Canadian Press, "Saskatchewan's Potash Royalty Structure."

53 Vardi, "Potash's $500 Million Man."

54 Mills, "Saskatchewan Losing Billions in Potash Royalties."

55 Pitts, "PotashCorp.'s Bill Doyle."

56 Marshall, *Saskatchewan Potash Taxes and Royalties*, 4.

57 Weir, "Privatizing Potash."

58 Chen and Mintz, "Fixing Saskatchewan's Potash Royalty Mess," 5.
59 Chen and Mintz, "Fixing Saskatchewan's Potash Royalty Mess," 5.
60 Chen and Mintz, "Fixing Saskatchewan's Potash Royalty Mess," 6.
61 MacPherson, "Sask. Potash Miners Not Sold on Royalty Review."

9. FIXING THE POTASH TAX PROBLEM

1 Saskatchewan Mining Association, *Saskatchewan Potash: A Snapshot of Saskatchewan's Potash Industry in 2020.*
2 MacPherson, "Sponsorship Inc."
3 PCS annual reports for this period.
4 MacPherson, "Sponsorship Inc."
5 PCS, *Making Plentiful Possible.*
6 Staples, "In Blame Game over High Food Costs."
7 Weir, "A Windfall Tax."
8 Weir, "A Windfall Tax." The amounts of profit mentioned here include all of Nutrien's profits (i.e., for potash, phosphates, nitrogen, and retail sales), whereas the numbers used in this book are for potash only, and therefore lower, and are also generally presented in Canadian dollars.
9 Weir, "A Windfall Tax."
10 Weir, "A Windfall Tax." Again, the figure used in this book is 16 percent and we are looking at a slightly different set of numbers. The point is the same either way.
11 Weir, "A Windfall Tax."
12 Saskatchewan Mining Association, *Saskatchewan Potash: A Snapshot of Saskatchewan's Potash Industry in 2021.*
13 Weir, "Privatizing Potash."
14 Nutrien, *Annual Report 2019,* 28.
15 Mintz's resume includes acting as advisor to the World Bank, acting as advisor to federal and provincial governments, serving on the board of Imperial Oil, holding various academic postings, and being CEO of the C.D. Howe Institute. He is a business-oriented individual, not given to flights of fancy or radical solutions.
16 Chen and Mintz, "Fixing Saskatchewan's Potash Royalty Mess."

10. CORPORATE WINDFALL, SASKATCHEWAN SHORTFALL

1 Fraser Institute, *Education Spending.*
2 Sanchez, *Saskatchewan Child and Family Poverty Report 2021,* 4.
3 Sanchez, *Saskatchewan Child and Family Poverty Report 2021,* 4.
4 Sanchez, *Saskatchewan Child and Family Poverty Report 2021,* 2.
5 Sanchez, *Saskatchewan Child and Family Poverty Report 2021,* 2.
6 Sanchez, *Saskatchewan Child and Family Poverty Report 2021,* 9.
7 Sanchez, *Saskatchewan Child and Family Poverty Report 2021,* 9.

8   Sanchez, *Saskatchewan Child and Family Poverty Report 2021*, 9.

9   Campaign 2000, *2022 Report Card on Child and Family Poverty in Canada*, 17.

10   Sanchez, *Saskatchewan Child and Family Poverty Report 2021*.

11   Sanchez, *Saskatchewan Child and Family Poverty Report 2021*, 3.

12   Salloum, "Landlord Association Says."

13   Salloum, "Landlord Association Says."

14   Salloum, "SIS Assistance Program."

15   Salloum, "SIS Assistance Program."

16   Salloum, "SIS Assistance Program."

17   Salloum, "SIS Assistance Program."

18   Salloum, "SIS Assistance Program."

19   Salloum, "SIS Assistance Program."

20   Saskatchewan Human Rights Commission, *Access and Equality for Renters*.

21   Wallace-Scribner, "Homeless in Regina."

22   Wallace-Scribner, "Homeless in Regina."

23   Cited in Ackerman, "Sask. Prof. Calls on Feds."

24   Gingrich and Rosenbluth, *$547 Million*.

25   Simpson, "For the Cost of Pharmacare."

26   Statistics Canada, 2016 Census.

27   Sachs, *The End of Poverty*, 299.

28   Plante, "The Costs of Poverty in Saskatchewan."

29   Malakieh, "Adult and Youth Correctional Statistics."

30   The Conference Board of Canada, *Education and Skills Report Card*.

31   Laidley and Tabbara, *Welfare in Canada*, 2020.

APPENDICES

1   See footnote to table 1.

2   Compiled from Saskatchewan Bureau of Statistics, Economic Review Excel
     Tables, Volume of Potash Production 1997–2021; Saskatchewan Ministry
     of Energy and Resources, Mineral Statistics Yearbook, 2008, 208–210; and
     Saskatchewan budget documents for 2022 and 2009–2022 as required.

BIBLIOGRAPHY

BOOKS

Blakeney, Allan. *An Honourable Calling*. Toronto: University of Toronto Press, 2008.

Burton, John. *Potash: An Inside Account of Saskatchewan's Pink Gold*. Regina: University of Regina Press, 2014.

Gruending, Dennis. *Promises to Keep: A Political Biography of Allan Blakeney*. Saskatoon: Western Producer Prairie Books, 1990.

Rediger, Pat. *The Crowns: A History of Public Enterprise in Saskatchewan*. Regina: Canadian Plains Research Centre, University of Regina, 2004.

Sachs, Jeffrey D. *The End of Poverty: Economic Possibilities for Our Time*. New York: Penguin Press, 2005.

ACADEMIC PAPERS, REPORTS, STUDIES, AND COMMISSIONS

Campaign 2000. *2022 Report Card on Child and Family Poverty in Canada— Pandemic Lessons: Ending Child and Family Poverty is Possible*. 2022.

Charlton, Ayden et al. *The Privatization of the Potash Corporation of Saskatchewan: A Case Study*. Regina: The Saskatchewan Institute for Social and Economic Alternatives, June 1996. As cited in Warnock, John W. *Exploiting Saskatchewan's Potash: Who Benefits?* Canadian Centre for Policy Alternatives, January 2011.

Chen, Duanjie, and Jack Mintz. "Fixing Saskatchewan's Potash Royalty Mess: A New Approach for Economic Efficiency and Simplicity." University of Calgary *School of Public Policy Research Papers* 6, no. 7 (February 2013).

Chen, Duanjie, and Jack Mintz. "Potash Taxation: How Canada's Regime Is Neither Efficient nor Competitive from an International Perspective."

University of Calgary *School of Public Policy Research Papers* 8, no. 1 (January 2015).

Christopher, Andrea S. "Single Payer Healthcare: Pluses, Minuses, and What It Means for You." *Harvard Health Blog*. Harvard Health Publishing (Harvard Medical School). June 27, 2016. health.harvard.edu/blog/single-payer-healthcare-pluses-minuses-means-201606279835.

The Conference Board of Canada. *Education and Skills Report Card*. June 2014.

Elferink, Maarten, and Florian Schierhorn. "Global Demand for Food is Rising. Can We Meet It?" *Harvard Business Review*. April 7, 2016.

Fattouh, Bassam. *Saudi Oil Policy: Continuity and Change in the Era of Energy Transition*. The Oxford Institute for Energy Studies Working Paper WPM81. January 2021.

Fraser Institute. *Education Spending in Public Schools in Canada, 2022 Edition*. October 6, 2022.

Gingrich, Paul, and David Rosenbluth. *$547 Million to Eliminate Poverty in Saskatchewan*. University of Regina oURspace. January 26, 2020.

Kurtzman, Laura. *Single-Payer Systems Likely to Save Money in US, Analyst Finds*. University of California, San Francisco. January 15, 2020.

Laidley, Jennefer, and Mohy Tabbara. *Welfare in Canada, 2020*. Caledon Institute of Social Policy and Maytree. December 2021. Revised May 2022.

Malakieh, Jamil. *Adult and Youth Correctional Statistics in Canada, 2018/2019*. Canadian Centre for Justice and Community Safety Statistics. December 21, 2020.

Marshall, Jim. *Saskatchewan Potash Taxes and Royalties: Is It Time for a Review?* University of Saskatchewan–University of Regina Johnson Shoyama Graduate School of Public Policy. January 2019.

Moore, Mark A., and Aidan R. Vining. *The Privatization of Potash Corporation of Saskatchewan*. Frontier Centre for Public Policy. February 2017.

Olewiler, Nancy. *The Potash Corporation of Saskatchewan: An Assessment of the Creation and Performance of a Crown Corporation*. Economic Council of Canada Discussion Paper no. 303. April 1986.

Organization of the Petroleum Exporting Countries. *2019 OPEC Annual Statistical Bulletin*.

Plante, Charles. "The Costs of Poverty in Saskatchewan (and How We Can Address Them)." Saskatchewan *Health Quality Council Blog*. December 19, 2019. saskhealthquality.ca/blog/the-costs-of-poverty-in-saskatchewan-and-how-we-can-address-them.

Romanow, Roy, J., Q.C. *Building on Values: The Future of Health Care in Canada*. Commission on the Future of Health Care in Canada (Government of Canada). November 2002.

Sanchez, Miguel. *Saskatchewan Child and Family Poverty Report 2021*. University of Regina Social Policy Research Centre. 2021.

Saskatchewan Human Rights Commission. *Access and Equality for Renters in Receipt of Public Assistance: A Report to Stakeholders.* 2018.

Silva, George. *Feeding the World in 2050 and Beyond—Part 1: Productivity Challenges.* Michigan State University Extension. December 3, 2018.

Thring, David E. "Alberta, Oil, and the Constitution." *Alberta Law Review* 17, no. 1. 1979.

MEDIA REPORTS

Ackerman, Jennifer. "Sask. Prof. Calls on Feds, Province to Take Action in High Child Poverty Rates." *Regina Leader-Post.* December 6, 2021.

Friedman, Gabriel. "BHP Accelerates Work on Its Saskatchewan Potash Mine as Prices Soar." *Financial Post.* July 19, 2022.

Giles, David. "Wall Blasts PotashCorp, Says Company Sacrificed Workers for Shareholders." Global News, Regina. December 5, 2013.

Hsieh, Esther. "What Norway Did with Its Oil and We Didn't." *The Globe and Mail.* May 16, 2013.

Ladurantaye, Steve. "Bill Doyle's Modest Return to Saskatoon." *The Globe and Mail.* February 23, 2011.

MacPherson, Alex. "The 100-Day War: An Oral History of BHP's Hostile Takeover Bid of PotashCorp." *Saskatoon StarPhoenix.* November 13, 2020.

MacPherson, Alex. "Premier Wall Says He Expects Head-Office Pledge to be Honoured After PotashCorp–Agrium Merger." *Saskatoon StarPhoenix.* August 31, 2017.

MacPherson, Alex. "Sask. Potash Miners Not Sold on Royalty Review." *Saskatoon StarPhoenix.* February 4, 2019.

MacPherson, Alex. "Sponsorship Inc.: What PotashCorp's Donations Mean to Saskatoon." *Saskatoon StarPhoenix.* January 28, 2017.

MacPherson, Alex. "Wall Pledges to Look at 'Every Option' to Enforce 2011 PotashCorp Pledge." *Saskatoon StarPhoenix.* September 6, 2017.

McCullough, Michael. "What Investors Still Don't Understand About Nutrien." *The Globe and Mail.* October 27, 2020.

McNish, Jacquie, Brenda Bouw, and Eric Reguly. "Potash: The Deal That Didn't Have to Die." *The Globe and Mail.* November 5, 2010.

Mills, Sarah. "Saskatchewan Losing Out on Billions in Potash Royalties: Mintz Report." *paNOW.* January 7, 2015.

Mintz, Jack M. "Brad Wall's Good Potash Play." *Financial Post.* March 24, 2015.

Mintz, Jack M. "The Potash Royalty Mess." *Financial Post.* October 14, 2010.

Peterson, Julia. "Deputy PM Visits, Touts Importance of Potash." *Saskatoon StarPhoenix.* August 25, 2022.

Pitts, Gordon. "PotashCorp.'s Bill Doyle Dims Hope for New Mines." *The Globe and Mail*. April 18, 2010.

"Potash Corp Urges Rejection of BHP Billiton's Bid." *BBC News*. August 23, 2010.

Salloum, Alec. "Landlord Association Says 30 Percent of SIS Clients Again Did Not Pay Rent in October." *Regina Leader-Post*. November 3, 2021.

Salloum, Alec. "SIS Assistance Program 'Not Working' Says Sask. Landlord Association." *Regina Leader-Post*. October 5, 2021.

Silcoff, Sean. "It Takes Chutzpah for Potash to Protest New Tax Regime." *The Globe and Mail*. March 19, 2015.

Simpson, Wayne. "For the Cost of Pharmacare, We Can Eradicate Poverty." *Financial Post*. November 21, 2019.

Staples, David. "In Blame Game over High Food Costs, Superstore Mogul Scores over NDP's Singh." *Edmonton Journal*. March 10, 2023.

The Canadian Press. "Saskatchewan's Potash Royalty Structure 'Alarmingly Inefficient': Report." *The Globe and Mail*. January 7, 2015.

Vardi, Nathan. "Potash's $500 Million Man." *Forbes*. August 19, 2010.

Wallace-Scribner, Tanner. "Homeless in Regina: Defining the Problem." 620 CKRM. March 20, 2023.

Weir, Erin. "Maximize Public Gain from Potash." *Saskatoon StarPhoenix*. September 3, 2010.

Weir, Erin. "Privatizing Potash Was a Costly Mistake." *Regina Leader-Post*. September 2, 2010.

Weir, Erin. "Time to Review Potash Royalties." *Saskatoon StarPhoenix*. February 10, 2011.

Weir, Erin. "A Windfall Tax to Fight Food Inflation—Not on Grocers but Commodity Producers." *The Globe and Mail*. April 11, 2023.

GOVERNMENT PUBLICATIONS

Government of Canada

Natural Resources Canada. *Gold Facts*. April 17, 2023 (updated February 17, 2023).

Natural Resources Canada. *Potash Facts*. January 16, 2020 (updated October 31, 2022).

Statistics Canada. 2016 Census of Population charts.

Government of Saskatchewan

Annual Budget Documents and Backgrounders, 1995–2003.

"Balanced Budget Keeping Saskatchewan Strong" (news release). March 18, 2015.

Economic Overview 2020.

Debates and Proceedings of the Legislative Assembly of Saskatchewan (*Hansard*). 18th Legislature, 1st Session. November 26, 1975. docs.legassembly.sk.ca/legdocs/Legislative%20Assembly/Hansard/18L1S/751126Debates.pdf.

Fuzesy, Anne. *Geological Report 181: Potash in Saskatchewan*. Saskatchewan Energy and Mines, 1982.

Journals of the Legislative Assembly of the Province of Saskatchewan vol. LXXX. Session, 1975–76.

Ministry of Energy and Resources, Mineral Statistics Yearbook, 2008.

"Potash Sector Sets New Records in Product and Sales in 2021" (news release). March 22, 2022.

"Premier Welcomes 'Pledge to Saskatchewan' from PotashCorp" (news release). February 14, 2011.

Saskatchewan Bureau of Statistics, Saskatchewan Provincial Economic Account, 2021; Economic Review 2021; and Economic Review Excel Tables, 1998–2021.

"Saskatchewan Potash Producers Ramp Up Production" (news release). June 22, 2022.

Saskatchewan's Dashboard on Business and Economy (Mineral Sales). Accessed March 8, 2022, and March 25, 2023.

Government of Norway

Norwegian Petroleum Directorate, Norwegian Ministry of Petroleum and Energy. "The Government's Revenues." Updated May 11, 2023. norskpetroleum.no/en/economy/governments-revenues.

CORPORATE DOCUMENTS

Annual Reports

Agrium Ltd. annual reports, and filings with US Securities and Exchange Commission

International Minerals and Chemical Corporation annual reports, and filings with US Securities and Exchange Commission

The Mosaic Company annual reports, and filings with US Securities and Exchange Commission

Nutrien annual reports, and filings with US Securities and Exchange Commission

Potash Corporation of Saskatchewan annual reports, and filings with US Securities and Exchange Commission

Other

IndexMundi. Potassium Chloride Monthly Price—US Dollars per Metric Ton.

Nutrien. *Providing Solutions for a Growing World: Sustainability Report 2018*. July 2019.

Potash Corporation of Saskatchewan Inc. *Making Plentiful Possible: Notice of Annual Meeting of Shareholders and Management Proxy Circular*. February 20, 2017.

Potash Corporation of Saskatchewan Inc. "PotashCorp's 'Pledge to Saskatchewan'" (news release). October 13, 2010.

Saskatchewan Mining Association. *Saskatchewan Potash: A Snapshot of Saskatchewan's Potash Industry in 2021.*

Saskatchewan Mining Association. *Saskatchewan Potash: A Snapshot of Saskatchewan's Potash Industry in 2020.*

The Mosaic Company. timetodigdeeper.com.

INDEX

Eric Cline practised law in his hometown of Saskatoon prior to serving sixteen years in the Saskatchewan legislature where he held several senior cabinet positions, including in health, finance, and industry and resources. After his time in politics, he worked for twelve years as a corporate executive in the mining sector before establishing an arbitration practice and working as a professional fused glass artist.